𝔍1

A Wondrous Story

To Be Told

VOLUME ONE

an attempt to retell the Bábí-Bahá'í Drama
in Iambic Pentameter, rhymed

by Kambeze B. Etemad

THE TALISMAN INSTITUTE

INDEED A WONDROUS STORY TO BE TOLD, Volume One
an attempt to retell the Bábí-Bahá'í Drama in Iambic Pentameter, rhymed

Published by the Talisman Institute
828 Morris Avenue, Bryn Mawr, PA 19010

Cover Photography: original film photos, and digital montage, by Kambeze B. Etemad

Publisher's Cataloging-in-Publication data
(Provided by Quality Books, Inc.)

   Etemad, Kambeze B., author.
     Indeed a wondrous story to be told. Volume one : an
   attempt to retell the Bábí-Bahá'í drama in iambic
   pentameter, rhymed / by Kambeze B. Etemad.
       pages cm
       ISBN 978-0-9976277-0-1 (paperback)
       ISBN 978-0-9976277-1-8 (hardback)
       ISBN 978-0-9976277-2-5 (ebook)

     1. Báb, 'Alí Muḥammad Shírází, 1819-1850--Poetry.
   2. Bahá'u'lláh, 1817-1892--Poetry. 3. Babism--Poetry.
   4. Babism--Biography. 5. Bahai Faith--Poetry. 6. Bahai
   Faith--Biography. I. Title.

   PS3605.T425I53 2016   811'.6
                                QBI16-1050

Printed in the United States of America

CONTENTS

CONTENTS

for Elyse

PREFACE

I hadn't read Shakespeare since high school.

Fast-forward 30 years to 2013.

In one of our only local brick-and-mortar bookstores, I came across a new book that was intriguing and irresistible, which would also appeal to my eight-year-old daughter Elyse, whose Star Wars fandom rivals (or surpasses) my own. It was *William Shakespeare's Star Wars* by Ian Doescher – a retelling of the original movie in iambic pentameter and other types of prose and poetry.

Bought it immediately, read it avidly.

Not only was it inherently cool, it was also a great inroad to Shakespeare for Elyse. And for me it was a reconnection to a type of English not experienced in three decades. Naturally, we gobbled it up, as we have Doescher's sequels.

This became for Elyse a springboard to some direct exposure to Shakespeare himself. And for myself it led to purchasing and reading a book of Shakespeare comedies, and a book of tragedies; they were a difficult but satisfying read.

From the beginning of this re-exposure to Shakespeare, I began experiencing something completely unexpected – even for someone who is a lover of words and word-play. I found myself quipping – and thinking – in rhymed iambic pentameter. Elyse was doing it too. It became a game, a new type of word-play for us.

Then it started – the experimenting. From some unexpected, totally amateur but joyfully playful zone within, I began to write. Not out of any aspiration to be a poet or any kind of literary something, but because it just seemed to come naturally. It carried a levity that was addictive. It seemed to capture many of the moments' thoughts and feelings, and it was just a lot of fun – especially within the context of our family life.

It started with a brief confession of the pentametric grips in which I found myself:

> Whenever I do read of Shakespeare's prose,
> my mind is naturally inclined, it goes
> to imitate his lofty language, do
> iambic and pentameter speak too.
>
> **Methinks In IP**   EarlyOct2013

Then a brief pre-bedtime quip for an always-alert Elyse who's reluctant to wind-down the day:

> For now it is the time to go to bed,
> upon the pillow lay thy sleepy head.
> Hygiene preceding then with reading, do
> I pray and sing then snuggle up with you.
>
> **Iambic Bedtime**   16Oct2013
>   with Elyse

A few very small blurbs trickled first.

Then some got a little longer.

Never were they a pretension to artistic output; they were simply a way of processing, internalizing and reflecting whatever was going on at the time - in a rhythm and rhyme that resonated within: ... from an extension of our daddy-daughter word-play (usually done in "normal" English, but now in the form of some short and silly rhyming "I.P.", as we began to refer to it) ... to an admission of my lazy exhaustion one Sunday morning ... from a longer avowal of love across the miles when Elyse and my wife Melanie were out of town ... to a medium sized, inadequate confession of inadequacy to Melanie for our 25th anniversary ...

Then came some narrative indulgences. The first narrative was a personal culmination of some homeschooling that had been going on for over a year. Driven by Elyse's avid interest, we as a family had been learning a lot about the American Revolution. This had been augmented by local visits to various historic sites in the Greater Philadelphia Area. And it culminated in two trips – first to Boston to see some of the early Revolutionary sites, then later to Virginia to explore Yorktown, Williamsburg and other places. The poem – "Pentametric Revolution" – was a personal way of synthesizing everything we had learned – as a primer for, and reflection of, our big trip to Virginia. It helped bring the entire Revolution and its significance to life during that trip.

Two other narrative works were essentially real-time journaling in IP of two separate family vacations to Florida. It was a different way of capturing beyond photographs, and engraving in memory, the highlights of each day of those trips – most especially the wonderment we all felt during our excursions to Harry Potter World at Universal Studios. It was such fun – even their titles were in iambic pentameter: "Our Magic Flor'da Fam'ly Escapade" and "Our Flor'da Fam'ly Escapade, Part Two."

This IP storytelling turned out to be a very satisfying and enjoyable release – reflective, playful, relaxing, journalistic, funny and invigorating all at the same time. Who knew?

One day sometime in early 2015, an idea came for another IP narrative project. But I told myself – "no... too big, totally beyond your wherewithal." But the idea kept coming back. Finally there was no resisting an attempt to combine this new storytelling mode with the narrative of my all-time favorite story. But the chosen story was huge, complex and archetypal. It was crazy to want to do this. In short, I found myself wanting to retell the true story of the Báb and Bahá'u'lláh in this amateur IP narrative style.

I had no idea what I was getting myself into.

I can't believe it's happened... have no idea how.

All there is to say is that I've had such a playful and satisfying time taking on this impossible adventure, and at the same time the experience has edified my deepest soul.

All this is being related to emphasize the following:

First: I am not a scholar or master of Shakespeare, literature, grammar, or even English. If you read this with the expectation that it's written with such expertise, you may very well be disappointed. That is not the point of this.

Second: I'm neither a scholar nor an expert on the Bahá'í Faith or its history. If you read this with the expectation that it's written with that kind of proficiency, you're again likely to be disappointed. And again, that's not the point of this.

My appeal to the reader is to keep in mind that the primal impulse behind the *writing* of this very amateur effort has been the love-joy-fun of combining a previously unseen creative curiosity (in this case, Shakespearean English) with a longstanding interest (in this case, a story of deep personal resonance).

This appeal also asks the reader to remember that the point of *sharing* this – if not just to divert – is to excite, in two ways. If this fusion provides a bridge between some readers and this Great History, and if it motivates them to more directly immerse themselves in the epochal and archetypal significance of the Wondrous Story it retells, then sharing it has served its primary "purpose."

A second "purpose" is that it might encourage some to explore their own unrefined artistry. If this project is anything, it's a testimony of the Layman's Odyssey to the Sublime – shared to excite anybody and empower everybody to welcome the utterly unexpected amateur creativity within themselves. If I can do this, then almost anyone is capable of the most unanticipated things.

FACTUAL NOTES

The synthesis and retelling of this Great Story are fundamentally informed by, and derive their historical veracity (and sometimes direct content) from the following references:

- *The Dawn-Breakers* – by Nabil

- *God Passes By* – by Shoghi Effendi

- *The Báb,* and *Bahá'u'lláh: King of Glory* – both by H.M. Balyuzi

- *The Revelation of Bahá'u'lláh* (Vols. 1-4) – by Adib Taherzadeh

- *Hour of the Dawn,* and *Day of Glory* – both by Mary Perkins

- *Release the Sun* – by William Sears

- *The Bahá'í Faith: Emerging Global Religion* – by Hatcher/Martin

Due to the exigencies of syllable, meter, rhythm and rhyme – in order to maintain iambic pentametric form – quotes of actual words spoken by the Báb, Bahá'u'lláh and other individuals were usually not verbatim. Most often, they were close approximations and adaptations; in such cases the meaning of the original quote was kept in the adaptation. When the quote was occasionally verbatim, it was purely serendipitous, and quite delightful.

Although this retelling is deeply and directly rooted in the genuine history found in the above references, it is still to be considered an artistic adaptation. This work, therefore, should not be considered a religious resource, an academic text, or a definitive accounting of what was said and done during that history.

As such, this retelling should in no way ever be considered a substitute for the reading of the authentic history found in the original sources by which it was inspired. Indeed, may this work excite the reader to dive directly and profoundly into those sources.

11

A NOTE ON TRANSLITERATION
of Persian and Arabic words

A pre-existing, standardized transliteration system was partially used and selectively applied for particular words (and not for others), as suited the interests of the author.

For an introduction to this system, see the online Wikipedia article on "Bahá'í Orthography."

VOLUME

ONE

the breaking of the Dawn of a new Day

Siyyid Alí-Muhammad is the Báb

Around the fire do come and we shall hear
a story – not of fiction, much more dear –
no fabled fantasy, but real and clear.
Though tragic, magic too, lives it'll steer –
illumine minds, and hearts will set afire.
Heroic actions from sublime desire
of Prophets, martyrs, saints – but not of old.
In Mid-East 1800's, story's told
of prophecy fulfilled, the old world dies –
with thousands, tens of thousands breaking ties
and living life a bold and novel way
as courage, love and truth break a New Day.
Across the generations to our time,
across the globe now millions join the rhyme.

Within this whole unfolding drama true
are Archetypes embedded through and through,
which manifest emblazoned, do beget
those precedents of virtue-challenge set.
The recapitulations have begun,
to be for generations that will come.

So open inner eye and inner ear,
and hearken to a story with no peer.
Imbibe and relish what is to unfold –
indeed a wondrous story to be told.

The matrix of our story is a clime
before Industr'al Revolution's time.
The 18th and the 19th centuries –
a fermentation of societies.

Political, religious power strained.
Mid-East to Europe and Amer'ca changed –
from revolutions to republics new,
and slowly fading empires that will rue.
Corruption and decay, the world it sees –
ecclesiastic and the monarchies.
The classic power balance Europe locks
with wars and rumored wars, a tinder box.
From slavery to subjugations rife,
to exploitations, economic strife,
disparities of wealth beyond our ken,
and women's rights unrecognized by men.
With conflict race and nationality,
religion-science full dichotomy,
fanaticism every type and form,
and ignorance of masses is the norm.

Within this dark-on-dark, it's hard to see
how hope of any kind there just might be.

Yet there it was: the expectations lie
in hearts of good-willed people, low and high:
the Age, the One awaited may be nigh.

From generations and from ages old,
across the centuries the hope retold.
In poet seer's vision it's foretold.
The sacred scriptures' prophecies are bold
from every faith tradition ever told:

from "Lord of Hosts come down," Judaic hope;
to "Christ returned in Father's glory" scope;
the "Great Announcement" in Islámic world –
for Sunní and for Shí'ih, wish unfurled
of "Mahdí" and "descent of Jesus Christ,"
"Husayn" and "12th Imám" blast "Trumpet" twice.
Transmitted age to age to culminate
in vergence 'round an 1800's date –
the "Promised One" will come and here abide.
The messianic expectation wide
in cities and across the countryside –
from Europe to the Middle-Eastern sand,
America and to the Holy Land.

The scholars and the people pray and wait.
Romantic thinkers, and the writers great –
like Shelley, Wordsworth – they anticipate
the Day, the Age, the One that will create
New Life, New World – their pens did celebrate.

And in the percolating dark and light,
Islámic Middle-East in thickest night.

The Persians in Írán – epitome
of such decline and sheer depravity:
the monarchy and clergy at the poles,
do rival and collude as they both dole
corruption and brutality so clear,
with ignorance, oppression – all in fear.

In such a corner dark, where hope is gone
does God enact the New Day's breaking Dawn.

The harbinger of this awaited time –

some 50 years before the Bell did chime.
Shaykh Ahmad from Arabia's northeast –
pure-hearted, pious, brilliant at least –
he studied what Islám was meant to be.
As mujtahid he gained authority,
but saw corruption and the strife within –
its shattered unity, its light gone dim,
its force as sapped, degraded was its name,
its purpose was perverted with no shame.

Resolv'd to counteract Islám's disease,
age 40 he forsook a life of ease.
Late 18th century began to teach
Qur'ánic allegoric truth to reach.

Renown'd with following did he create,
while others envy, malice and with hate.

Kept on did Ahmad, though he'd quickly see:
complete reform within Islám won't be.
And only will a Revelation new,
Divine and independent ever do.

So delving in the Qur'án and Hadíth ,
discerned he all the Mahdí's prophecies.
And to a chosen inner circle of
disciples, with perception and with love
did he relate the pending advent of
the promised Revelators from above.

While travel-teaching, came he to Shíráz,
and praised it as a one-day new Hijáz.

Then meeting a new student shining bright –
so young and singular and erudite –
Ahmad did Siyyid Kázim trust complete
to save the Shaykhí movement from defeat.
Unfolded everything to Kázim's mind
and deputized him: Shaykhís teach in kind –
allowing Ahmad meditation more,
and larger matters to address, explore.

An homage to Tihrán as they pass through,
allude to "Alí" passed from old to new.
Discerning his own end, Ahmad he knows:
appoint succession to Kázim, then goes.

Siyyid Kázim for 17 more years
continues teaching to the hearing ears
the outer general allegory truth
and inner pending promise of the Youth.

He clarifies that promise is for *two*:
two Revelations will the world renew.
"The first will be the Qá'im of your quest;
then after, the Qáyyúm will manifest."
Twin trumpet blasts, two promised Ones to come –
with signs and names to recognize each one.
Especially the first One to arrive –
prepare receptive souls did Kázim strive.

Occasion once, while teaching he had been,
a most amazing Visitor came in –
unrecognized by all but our Kázim
who, speechless and entranced by godly Gem,
could not attempt continuing to teach;
perhaps by cryptic gestures, hearts to reach.

A few short days before, in very truth,
Kázim had paid a visit to this Youth –
attaining to his inmost heart's desire
with mystic interaction, soul afire.

And yet our Siyyid Kázim had no lack
of those who gave resistance and attack
from fear and envy of his truth and reach.
Supporters he would need to help him teach.

Among the brightest for the Shaykhí fame:
the brill'ant poetess, Qurratu'l-'Ayn.

Plus deputy for key endorsements' gain:
intrepid teacher was Mullá Husayn.

And as that travel teacher was away,
a shepherd Siyyid Kázim met one day.

A dream the shepherd had, and now must tell
to naught but Siyyid Kázim, as a knell.

The Prophet had appeared within the dream
with news that would be sad, so it would seem –
assuring of Kázim's impending death,
but this brought joy to Kázim's every breath.

Though all disciples mourned the sudden news,
the Siyyid said: "Rejoice! These are the cues:
my passing indicates the time has come,
for you shall soon behold the Promised One!
So scatter far and wide when I am gone,
search everywhere to find the breaking Dawn.
Invoke the help of God, your quest be won.
Don't stop until you've found the Promised One."

So when Mullá Husayn did then return –
his master gone, disciples all a-churn –
he asked what last instructions had been said.
They told him; and then Mullá Husayn said:

"Then wherefore have you tarried here so long?
Why not are all of you far and wide gone?"

"We dare not leave," they said, "we must close ranks;
we will accept your leadership with thanks.
Indeed, were you to claim to be the One
our master promised, no objections – none."

"Nay! God forbid!" he said to this request.
"Forthwith I shall make prep to go on quest,
that Siyyid Kázim's final words are done,
and go search everywhere for Promised One."

Then Mullá Husayn did for forty days
seclude himself, fast, meditate and pray –
prepared himself and sharpened inner sight,
attuned his soul to then be guided right.

Then set off, with companions did he go
on dusty roads – to where he did not know.

A long and ardent journey did begin.
Intuitively magnet-drawn he'd been
toward Shíráz – of rose and poet fame.
At last arriving there, without a name,
at quiet eventide, without a claim –
hot, tired, at the gate, with no fanfare,
anonymously dirty, needing fare.

Then Mullá Husayn supplicates in pra'er.
Behold! A Stranger was approaching there!

Green turban and a face of radiant joy,
embrace of loving welcome, no alloy:
a Youth of 25 and so refined –
how did He know to come that place and time?

Alí-Muhammad was His given name –
a merchant and a siyyid, quiet fame.
Invited Husayn to His modest home
to rest from all the roads that he did roam.
With joyful wonder Mullá Husayn went
for wash and tea and prayer, time was spent.

The Host was ever mild and dignified.
Warm hospitality was all inside.

Then conversation started 'twixt the two.
The Host would ask, the guest replying to:

"Who are you?"

"Student of Siyyid Kázim."

"Who leads the Shaykhís now?"

" 'Twill be Qá'im."

"Distinctive features of the Promised One?"

The guest described them each now, one by one.

Then Host, while calm, with vibrant voice said He:

"Behold, these signs are manifest in Me."

Delineating how each sign applied
to His own Person, further He replied.

A stagg'ring claim for One unknown and young;
a deeply cosmic test had just begun.
But who is being tested – Host or guest?
Is claimant or criteria the best?

A startled Mullá Husayn vacillates
from bold insistence on to terror's gates.

To posit questions is his only goal –
to quiet, modest, most entrancing Soul.

Criteria that Mullá Husayn brought
were of two kinds, within his heart he sought:
the first, his own scholastic inquiries;
the second, secret proof of mysteries
predicted by Siyyid Kázim to seal:
unask'd, the Qá'im will for him reveal
a commentary on a Súrih prime,
a gift to him and also for all time.

So Mullá Husayn started with the first;
he lost his words, though they were well-rehears'd;
so treatise he had written, question-filled;
he asked the Host to comment, if He willed.

The Mystic Host, He quickly glanced the book,
then answered Mullá Husayn, whose soul shook.
Resolving every question, minutes' time –
advancing far beyond to themes sublime.
The guest, he was amazed by potent words,
and thrown in tempest by what next he heard:

"Don't test Me by your standards," said Alí;
"they're naught to the Reality in Me;
and it's the other way – for God tests thee."

"Now is the time," Alí said sans appeal,
"the Súrih's commentary to reveal."

He took up pen, and with exquisite hand
wrote quickly, unpremeditated, and
He chanted as He wrote out every strand.

"This night, this ho-ur, in the days to come" –
did say the Host – "a celebrated one."
Then after dinner, more revealing done.

The guest was by the voice of Host enthrall'd,
and spellbound by His utterance, which called
to dazzling heights of knowledge and insight.
Oblivious of time he was that night –
and Mullá Husayn's thunderstruck a time.
Then ecstasy was broke by morning sign.

Alí-Muhammad then said pointedly:
"O thou who art the first to b'lieve in Me,
I am the Báb, the Gate of God, ver'ly."

As hist'ry from the past awaits His Name,
so hist'ry now will never be the same.

forsooth, the Báb to our tale is not new.
The harbingers indeed already knew
but kept it secret – nothing else would do.

For decades prior, Shaykh Ahmad did see
exchange of his lost son for this Alí.

It also was the Báb who had been quite
the Host to Siyyid Kázim's magic night,
and visited that class at teaching's height
to render Kázim speechless with delight.

In Shíráz 1819, born was He –
respected siyyid merchant family.

From early, unlike any other child:
pure, sweet, serene, plus courteous and mild,
kind, humble, handsome, tender-hearted, bright,
astounding wisdom, knowledge and insight,
melodic chanting rapturous delight.

He started at the local school, age five –
astonished teacher, brill'ance uncontrived;
the teacher put Him back in fam'ly hands
and said, "He, in no need of teacher stands."
"Like other pupils, be" uncle restates,
but irrepressible is Light innate.

Extr'ordinary knowledge does astound
the older theologic students 'round.
And meditating often, also pra'er.
A fond affection for Him everywhere.

At 15 started working fam'ly trade.
A stellar merchant reputation made:
His truthfulness and humble dignity,
and scrupulously fair integrity,
attention to detail, and charity –
expressions of His devout piety.

A quiet married life at 23 –
where tender kindness, love, affection be –
with Khadíjih-Bagum, whose heart could see
through dreams her husband's high Sublimity.

At 24, one night He dreamed His Soul
was permeated and was taken whole
by Spirit of God; it had been possessed
by Presence of Divine – heart's thrill'd unrest;
and myst'ries of God's Revelation did
unfold to eyes of Alí, now unhid.

Then waking Revelations did begin –
ecstatic meditations seizing Him.

One night Khadíjih accident'lly spied
Alí in waking rapture – tears He cried,
His face is luminous, and from it streams
the rays of light while chanting lofty themes.
It was no accident, but God allowed
Khadíjih to this witness, so no doubt
within her heart, as she is first to see
God's Manifestation is her Alí.

Then shortly after this, Mullá Husayn
the first disciple of the Báb became –
May 23rd of 1844,
the turning point of what had gone before.

The Báb told Mullá Husayn: "tell no one."
For eighteen independently must come,
embrace Him through their own determined ways.

And so it was within those heightened days,
seventeen more the Báb they did embrace –
through vision, dream, or see it in His face.

Among them was the great Qurratu'l-'Ayn,
who never met the Báb, yet all the same ...
she's fearless, clever, beautiful to see,
a vision of the Báb in dream had she,
and wrote a poem-pledge preemptively,
to be delivered to the Báb by one
who was among the sixteen more to come.

One night, the Báb to Husayn said discreet:
"One more, the chosen number to complete.
Tomorrow night, remaining one will come,
then chosen number of disciples done."

Next evening as the two of them did walk,
a Shaykhí youth – most humble, modest talk –
divinely guided, dusty, travel-stained –
approaching, caught sight of the Báb, exclaimed:

"I recognize Him by His very gait!
For none but He, to be the Truth, can state.
None manifests the pow'r and majesty
that radiateth from His Person – see!"

Astonished, Husayn to the Báb he told.
The Báb said, "Marvel not at action bold.
In world of spirit We've communed with him.
Indeed, await his coming; summon him."

Of all disciples, followers we'll see –
most knowing, potent and perceiving's he.
"Quddús" his new name from the Báb will be.

These ready souls, disciples each and all –
the "Letters of the Living" they were called –
were gathered by the Báb, each with a task,
a last time in His Presence they would bask.

Instructions for them all to promulgate
at last the advent of the Promised Gate.
Identity, do not reveal just yet,
but make it clear the Qá'im you have met.

Before He sent them all upon their way,
to all His Letters did the Báb then say:

"You are the bearers of God's name this Day.

This is the advent of a mighty Day.

Repositories chosen – this you are.

And righteous deeds and attributes go far.

So scatter throughout length and breadth of land,

prepare the way for coming of Him, and

heed not your weaknesses and fra-il-ty,

arise in His name, wholly trusting be,

and be assured of ult'mate victory."

The Living Letters, they all left – but two,
with unique roles for both of them to do.

'Twas Mullá Husayn and Quddús who stayed,
to whom the Báb confided and plans made.

The first great act the Báb would undertake:
Islám's heart: His announcement He would make.

Before embarking, He would want a sign;
that task to Mullá Husayn did assign.
The Báb gave him a mission thus defined:

"I shall direct your steps to city which
enshrines a Mystery transcendent, which
Hijáz nor this Shíráz its holiness
can hope to rival."   And to move this quest:
"The power's essence, dwelling now in you.
I won't go to Hijáz till hear from you."
So Mullá Husayn left, this task to do.

Encounters disappointing on the way,
till youth from town of Núr he met one day,
who verified to our Mullá Husayn
that there was Someone from that town whose name
for character and intellect and charm,
and art and virtue, loving-kindness warm,
attainments were by all acknowledged true;
discons'late cheers, and feeds the hungry too.

Befriending poor and stranger is His height.
Roams woods, in country beauty He delights.
Husayn-Alí – that is His given name.
It brought delight to our Mullá Husayn
each detail of this noble Man to heed
and that the Núrí youth knows Him indeed.

Then Mullá Husayn to the youth, a plea
to take a letter to Husayn-Alí,
some Writings of the Báb for Him to see,
report back with result immed'ately.

Husayn-Alí, upon perusing Words,
did instantly and openly was heard,
acknowledge Source and Origin Divine,
endorse the Báb in utterance sublime.

Through Núrí youth did Husayn-Alí send
a gift to Mullá Husayn, who did end
his almost inarticulate delight
with words to Núrí youth that special night:

"Tell no one of this, now is not the time;
downtrodden He'll exalt, the Bell will chime;
enrich the poor, redeem the fallen too –
till then this Secret keep, enjoining you."

Significance of this Husayn-Alí
would for some time remain a Mystery.

But from the start, the Báb did clearly see;
and clear it would become to history.

The Báb did correspond regularly –
communicating with Husayn-Alí
throughout the course of His whole ministry.

In all the Writings of the Báb, we see
a tone of full divine authority ...
except His letters to Husayn-Alí –
with serv'tude, sacrifice, humility.

More later there's to come, as we shall see.
For now, suffice to say, Husayn-Alí
was sought at Báb's instructions verily –
first order of the Báb's priority,
delaying trip to Mecca till does He
receive endorsement from Husayn-Alí,
and then can start His public ministry.

The Báb receives word from Mullá Husayn:

Husayn-Alí's endorsement of His claim.
Great joy to heart of Báb did ver'ly flow.
Immed'ately makes prep for trip, to go
to Mecca and Medina, pilgrim way.

For long Shí'ih tradition, it does say
that Promised One, announce Himself He will
in Mecca at the Ka'bih, to fulfill.

So Quddús as compan'on the Báb chose,
to join the massive people river flows
of multitud'nous pilgrims to Hijáz.
Together did they set out from Shíráz.

Two months of journey difficult, endure
on boat then camel – unsafe and unsure.

Despite discomforts – peaceful and content
to meditate and pray their time is spent,
and Revelation throughout as they went.

At sea the voyage got quite rough at times
so that the Báb did God beseech betimes
for ocean travel safer, easier;
indeed soon after shipping changes stir.

On land while camelback the Báb did ride,
Quddús would chant and guard and walk beside.

While stopp'd at desert well for rest and pra'ers,
an Arab Bedouin thief boldly dares –
absconds with saddlebag that does contain
the Writings of the Báb! Will none remain?
The servant of the Báb begins a chase.
While still in pra'er, the Báb, He indicates
the chase abandon; He would later say
that through the Arab and his chosen way,
those Writings now will destined places gain
that they themselves could surely not attain;
decreed by God this was, content remain.

In Mecca now, with ten days' pilgrim rite,
a great crowd 'round the Ka'bih – marv'lous sight.

Against the Ka'bih now the Báb does stand,
on ring upon its door He holds His hand,
He calls out clearly with Divine Command:

"I am that Qá'im,"

He did boldly call,

"Whose advent you have been awaiting all!"

Three times He sounded this to those in thrall.

A sudden hush upon these stirring words –
as if the throng of pilgrims, once they heard
this thunderclap in world of Islám's heart,
did stop and reset, now they can restart.

Then many took the news home of this claim.
Forthwith did others there accept His Name.

As well, the Báb a letter He did write
to Mecca's own sherif, so that He might
articulate His claims and message there.
Sherif too busy, didn't read or care.

To Shaykhí leader there, the Báb did call
a challenge; and the Shaykhí did forestall.

From Mecca to Medina did they go,
so homage to the Prophet they could show.

As well, the Báb did want to visit, pray
at shrine of Shaykh Ahmad, who there did lay.

Returning to Írán, they did arrive
in Búshihr, summer 1845.

The Báb, He stays; sends Quddús on ahead
back to Shíráz with Writings to be read:
a treatise of devotional new deeds
for growing group of followers to heed.

Quddús was chosen as the Báb's right hand,
and now the Báb gave Quddús a command:
accept their separation till the end;
his destiny this great Cause to defend,
invested with a power to astound,
enkindle seekers, enemies confound.

𝕭efore the 𝕭áb returnéd to Shíráz,
the town and province already abuzz.

Indeed by now across Írán is there,
through teaching by the Bábís' boldly dare,
a stirring of the people everywhere.

from first day that the Living Letters went,
toward Iráq was Mullá Alí sent;
he couldn't wait to openly proclaim,
so beaten in Shíráz for sounding claim.

Iráq to Karbilá his early aim,
and thereby soon did meet Qurratu'l-'Ayn;
a copy of Báb's commentary gave
to her and town divines with spirit brave.

In eager int'rest Karbilá did whir;
she taught with force, the streets and places stir;
embrace did many Shaykhís 'cause of her.

Divines opposing on their own behalf
as Mullá Alí's heading to Najaf.
When there, at gathering does he announce;
a heretic by clergy he's denounced.

The Ottoman authorities are called;
to prison in Baghdád is he installed;
his teaching in the prison makes a stir;
Constantinople prison, a transfer.
Privations of the body overwhelm –
succumbing, wings his flight to other realm.

The first to suffer for the Cause was he.
All honor to the young Mullá Alí.

Qurratu'l-'Ayn's already light and fire
before the Bábí Cause did her inspire.

Her fam'ly, filled with clergy do we find.
Her beauty only rivaled by her mind.
Acknowledg'd everyone: none like her kind,
and moreso in that Age for womankind –
her knowledge gen'ral and religious themes;
poetic prodigy, artistic streams;
a fearless love for justice, and forsooth
though still in veil, outspoken for the truth.

Her voice unstill'd, the family men perturb'd.
To let her speak but keep life undisturbed,
from curtain's cover she would be allowed
t'expound on topics to a lofty crowd –
confounding priests and scholars with her words,
astounding those her poetry had heard.

Becoming Shaykhí, fam'ly she defies.
It focuses her light, and it will rise.

Her dreaming of the Báb, to see His face –
a Living Letter role she does embrace,
exalting her capacities sublime,
distressing fam'ly men and the divines.

And public teaching, even in the street –
that many who Qurratu'l-'Ayn did meet
became Bábís – from lowly to elite.

Mullá Husayn had gone to Isfáhán,
where some embraced and others want him gone.
Káshán the same, while Qum did not respond.
Opposing Shaykhí leader in Tihrán.

But student of that Shaykhí was indeed
the one to help with Mullá Husayn's need
for sought endorsement from Husayn-Alí.

Then to Mashhad and then to Khurásán
to sow first seeds had Mullá Husayn done.
Then to Iráq, await Báb's word to come.

𝒜rriving in Búshihr, come from Hijáz,
the Báb sends Quddús onward to Shíráz.

When Quddús there arrives, he first explains
to uncle of the Báb his Nephew's claims.
Wholeheartedly accepting this new Name,
this uncle's utter service – future fame.

A certain Mullá Sádiq, Quddús tells.
Sádiq does fully fall under the spells,
forthwith enacts the Báb's devotion deeds,
particularly one for all to heed:
revised adhán-call did the Báb compose –
Alí-Muhammad's station in it rose.
At Muslim call to prayer, Sádiq clear
did chant the new adhán for all to hear.

Of heresy accuséd Sádiq was.
Disorder, turmoil all throughout Shíráz –
exacerbating province anarchy
and civil unrest there'bouts already,
for which a gov'nor new, one Husayn Khán,
for his brutality known through Írán.

From clergy pressure and his own device,
Bábís' arrest and inquisition. Twice
a punishment: first, piercing through the nose
and cord run through, leash-lead through town by foes.

They did this to Sádiq and to Quddús.
Then secondly, on top of this abuse,
900 lashes onto Sádiq's back.
Though body frail, he bore this harsh attack
with joy and with indifference to amaze;
he said that after seventh lash did blaze,
an exultation just took over then
both soul and body, 'twas no pain again.

Then both were from Shíráz expelled in turn,
with crucifixion threat if they return.

The hateful gov'nor did not leave it there.
The Báb's arrest he ordered in Búshihr,
to Shíráz to be brought back clad in chains,
to quell this Movement by its Source defame.

The Báb, He knew, anticipating fate.
Went up to soldiers who did hesitate,
He offered to go easy and not flee
to expedite the task of soldiery
and serve their need to governor obey.
His charm and honor won their hearts that day.

And by the time to Shíráz gate they came,
they gave their hearts to Him now, unrestrained.
The regiment did follow rev'rently
the Báb, Who did arrive in majesty –
a wonderment for all Shíráz to see.

Infuriated, Husayn Khán was bold
and publicly the Báb did rudely scold.

The Báb did quote Qur'án with no delay –
chastising in return the gov'nor's way.

And then the Báb was struck with hateful force –
His turban falling to the ground in course.

The chief Mullá, ashamed by gov'nor's deeds,
instead did ask some civil inquiries.

To which the Báb replied and made it clear
He did not claim to be – before nor here –
the intermediary, nor again
the representative of the Qá'im.

His most astute response did quell the rage,
while also serving as His sounding stage
to say to all who had the ears to hear
He was not go-between, but much more dear –
not proxy, but the Qá'im manifest.
For many, quiet joy; for others, test.

His uncle posted bail, on house arrest –
with many visitors for three day fest.

Then after that just fam'ly many weeks,
strict limitation of who with Him speaks.

And meanwhile throughout Persia, much the same:
disciples raising call and stating Name.
Aborting Karbilá, to Isfáhán
does Mullá Husayn teach within Írán.
Quddús to Yazd, then Isfáhán, Káshán,
then tries in Qum, then onward to Tihrán.
And others too, a wave across Írán.

Shíráz is seething, full of stories now.
Divines are clamoring for action now –
insist the Báb within the mosque appear,
recant His claim and make position clear,
in public fashion, everyone to hear.

Tremendous throng did fill the mosque, and more –
the cloisters, courtyard, rooftops, also more –
that even minarets spectators had,
to witness for themselves: divine or mad?

The Báb is now escorted to the scene –
exalted bearing, robe, and turban green.

The dignity and power, they did shine.
The silent scene as if it were a shrine.

Ascending pulpit, He then turns around,
the people strain their ears to miss no sound.

The Báb begins to speak with eloquence
for thirty minutes, soulful resonance.

Astounding talk on Unity Divine
in Arabic with fluency sublime,
enrapturing the people in that time.

Then rudely interrupted by a priest,
He then addresses question, now released:

"I speak what spoke the Messenger of God,
and don't speak what my Grandfather did not."

And then two core traditions did He quote
to challenge those perceiving to take note:

"Until the Day of Resurrection comes,
the lawful from Muhammad lawful runs,
and what He did forbid, forbidden runs."

"Whenever the Qá'im arises – see:
the Day of Resurrection that will be."

The Báb descended pulpit and did stare
a-face-to-face to rude priest standing there.

Then back to home, escorted by the guard,
while meaning of His words did all regard –
reiterating double-purpose words
to calm the deaf and thrill the ones who heard.

The opposite effect had clerics' plan.
Of this event the word spread, nay it ran.
To those perceiving, sure the Báb did claim
God's Messenger He was, Qá'im He came.
The ignorant appeased by language veiled,
believers strengthened as the truth prevailed.

And new disciples start the ranks to swell.
The clergy say it's time to sound the knell.
Death sentence is proclaimed and they do sign.
Imám-Jum'ih, though, vetoes their design.
And quiet house arrest imposed for time.

𝔄𝔩𝔩𝔬𝔴'𝔡 were secret visits to arrange
from several teachers, e'en Mullá Husayn.

The Báb would give instructions; Writings too –
both already revealed, plus Verses new
that constantly stream down like pouring rain.
The revelations of the Mystic Fane
did steadily and lib'rally descend
all during these times and between events –
infusing with new power the Báb's Being,
to radiate it out to everything,
with Verses new divine accompan'ing.

These teachers then dispersed across the land –
new waves of inquiry and teaching spanned
the provinces of Persia; they proclaim
His name, His claim, identity made plain;
distributing His Verses, they unbind
His teachings, leaving the old world behind –
His Word and Spirit catching mind to mind.

Now enter role of royal power brutes.
The Shah, the King, has power absolute,
with sycophants and ministers corrupt.
A savage legal – justice does disrupt.

The desp'rate masses – poverty or less.
Minority possessing wealth excess.

Prime Minister, the Grand Vazir we see
is one called Haji Mirza Aqasi,
who had the greatest power in the land,
and wielded it with arbitrary hand.
Though cunning, limited ability,
and eas'ly threatened by his jealousy,
was overbearing, with false piety,
misgoverned realm with prideful treachery.
Fanatical and bigoted and cruel
and hateful and corrupt; his crowning jewel:
society oppressed in misery,
with discontent throughout the land we see.

So in this context we appreciate
reaction to the Bábí Movement great.

When news of Bábís, Shíráz and the Báb
do reach the court and hearing of the Shah,
afraid is Haji Mirza Aqasi.
But to his credit, does the Shah decree
an envoy to investigate the One
Who's at the center of this – what's He done?

He chose Siyyid Yahyáy-i-Dárábí –
most famous, learned, eloquent is he.
With judgment excellent and knowledge deep,
the Shah in him a total faith does keep.
So Siyyid Yahyá's verdict will be key
to how the King responds to Báb, Alí.

Siyyid Yahyá received in honor was
by Husayn Khán the gov'nor in Shíráz.
In pride and skill he planned his bold intent
to overcome the Báb in argument.

With testing questions – difficult, obscure –
to their first meeting went he feeling sure;
he rattled off the questions in his stride.
The Báb did listen calmly, then replied.

Now Siyyid Yahyá marveled at the Words;
the answers brief and clear is what he heard.

The ease with which the Báb spontan'ously
did give reply to pre-planned inquiry
amazéd Siyyid Yahyá; 'twas no game:
the proud bright envoy now felt lowly shame.

A second set of questions, more sincere,
as second interview was drawing near.

And at that meeting, Yahyá felt so blind
as all his questions vanished from his mind.
Bewildered by forgetting all his thoughts,
was moreso when provided all he sought:
the Báb then brief, in language with no peer,
unask'd did answer every question clear.

When Siyyid Yahyá from this meeting left,
confused and of his confidence bereft.

In awe, he question'd his ability:
in every situation, surely he
comports self with aplomb and dignity –
with scholars, clergy and nobility,
and even in the court of royalty –
he's always brightest light in room to see;
so why a child in panic does he be
in company of this young Shírází?
So then he mustered in humility.

He wants last interview with different start,
and harbors one last question in his heart:
a wish to hear a commentary new
on a specific Súrih, with no clue:
he would not ask the Báb for it in word.
A silent test: the Báb his spirit heard?
If this unspoken wish the Báb did grant,
then Siyyid Yahyá would his pride recant.

Third interview, on entering the room,
great fear did seize the envoy, he did swoon.

The Báb does gently steady him, and then
He talks with loving tone and mystic ken.

The following He says:
                              "Seek verily
whatever is your heart's desire from Me.
I will reveal it to you readily."

Now Siyyid Yahyá, dumbstruck heart and head;
and so the Báb continued, and He said:

"Were I the commentary to reveal
for you on Súrih that you wish, unseal,
would you acknowledge that My Words are born
of Spirit God, and cease to be so torn?"

Then Siyyid Yahyá does begin to weep
from awe and feelings, w'in he could not keep.

The Báb does solace give, the heart to heal;
then does begin to wondrously reveal
in unpremeditated verses – write
spontaneously, leading to delight
of Siyyid Yahyá who recounts the sight:
'Twas "inexpressible" the "majesty,"
as well "astounding" the "rapidity,"
as "verses streamed from pen," makes one rejoice.
And the "soft gentle murmur of His voice,"
the "force stupendous of His style," did too
bewilder and amaze the envoy through.
No pause in revelation did occur
until the fullness of the verses were
completed and the commentary done.
The Báb then called for tea; it was begun.

When finished, then the Writing read aloud,
and moreso was the envoy's spirit wowed
by "accents" said "unutterably sweet;"
his "heart leapt madly" when it there did meet
the "treasures" that were in those words "enshrined."
He stayed three nights at home of Host Divine;

he copied book, the references did check –
Traditions and Qur'án citations check.

Without a single error, the Báb's work;
delighted was Yahyá to be His clerk.
And utterly convinced he ver'ly was
of Source Divine, that manifest it does
in heart-mind of the Báb there in Shíráz.

And thus does Yahyá's testimony start:
"No one but God can captivate my heart;
and who can thus ensnare, He is forsooth
of God, and His words are the Voice of Truth."

The gov'nor now is angry at Yahyá,
who meets no longer with the 'Ulamá.
Both gov'nor and the envoy write the Shah.

The King tells Haji Mirza Aqasi:
"Siyyid Yahyá has become a Bábí.
It us behooves, belittling to cease
the Cause of that Siyyid, allow Him peace."

The Báb gives Siyyid Yahyá a new name:
the title "Vahíd" hist'ry pens his fame.

Now Vahíd travels wide from town to town
and teaches strong, the Bábí Cause renown.

When **Vahíd's news** to town of Zanján went,
one Muslim teacher, leader prominent
did make arrangements to, without restraint,
with claim and Writings of the Báb acquaint.

This teacher of Zanján was quite renowned.
A lucid, fluent, forceful voice he owned.
Outspoken and quite knowledgeable true,
direct and independent-minded too.

As soon as verses of the Báb read he,
forthwith he testify did publicly
that verses streaming from the Báb hereon
proceed from Source the same as the Qur'án.
And openly, allegiance did he pledge
unto the Báb, and never did he hedge.

Another travel teacher he became,
and from the Báb, "Hujjat" was his new name.

Majority of Shaykhis did embrace.

All walks and strata of the human race
within Íránian society –
from sifter of wheat to nobility,
from backbone of the merchant class they came,
to humbly bold divines – took up the claim.

The wi-ld fi-re spread throughout the land –
the conscience of the masses stirring, and
provoking fearful hateful clergy's hand.

A year of house arrest does not deter
the impact of the Báb to still occur.
Considerable influence has He,
as gov'nor's spies do regularly see.

Despite Husayn Khán's efforts to degrade,
the reputation of the Báb is made
by eager crowds each night outside His home –
His grace and wisdom shower those who roam.

It's also noted by the Grand Vazir,
who also keeps his own spies ever-near,
in ever-growing jealousy and fear.

One night, obeying governor's command,
Chief Constable into the house breaks, and
arrests the Báb – with plan to execute.
But Constable's perceptions are acute.
An outbreak of the cholera in town;
the people flee in terror all around.
Processional of coffins he does see;
from gov'nor's mansion everyone did flee.
The Constable to home he makes a run,
discovering the news of dying son;
he begs the Báb, repents and post resigns,
and to His Mercy his own son consigns.

The Báb gives water for the boy to drink,
and soon the boy's no longer at the brink.

Upon his son's recovery, the Chief
does write the governor with full belief,
convincing Husayn Khán to spare his own
by ceasing to harass the Báb, atone.

The Báb, He is released by Husayn Khán,
but banished from Shíráz to Isfáhán.

Predicts He to His uncle, time will come
they'll meet in mountains of Ádhirbáyján.

Now even though the Báb, He did move on,
the cruelty did not stop from Husayn Khán.
Some threats and fines and torturing did he
of Bábís and the Báb's own family.

And northward, Fall of 1846,
three hundred miles, a destination fixed,
the Báb did travel from His Shíráz home.
To Isfáhán – the city of the domes
and palm and fruit trees, colleges and mosques,
the capital of faméd Shah Abbás,
with palaces and gardens so sublime,
and erudition of Shí'ih divines.

Indeed, the Governor of Isfáhán:
a diff'rent kind of man than Husayn Khán.
Though harsh and sometimes brutal, also fair;
a tott'ring province did he thus repair.
To history, his name: Manúchihr Khán –
a Georgian Christian slave, comes to Írán;
he's raised a Muslim, but he's not convinced
of Prophet's mission or what He evinced.
An able soldier, battles for the King.
In many parts of Persia – uprising,
and Manúchihr that region pacifies.
In public service also does he rise:

his method sometimes cruel, but seen as just –
protecting weak, a region he'd adjust
and therein bring security. With name
as kingdom's best administrator fame,
serves faithfully, most trusted by the Shah –
and thus rewarded by the King: did draw
a most respected posting in Írán
as Governor of Province Isfáhán.

The Báb a letter writes to Manúchihr
to ask where He might stay while exiled there.
The letter's penmanship and courtesy
impress'd the Governor so much that he
a special escort does arrange to go
accompany the Báb and honor show.

Then at the home of Chief Mullá, a Guest.
That Mullá by the Báb is so impress'd,
he personally sees to all His needs,
and humble service to the Báb, his deeds.

Distinguished learned clergy start to come
in numbers, thus to visit and become
acquainted with the Báb, and also see
at home of Chief Mullá, where stay does He.

One night while many guests were gathered 'round,
the Chief Mullá does ask the Báb t'expound –
a Qur'án chapter's comment'ry reveal.
At once the Báb obliges this appeal,
takes pen and paper and begins to write,
unstopping till He finishes that night –
then chants the treatise, to the group's delight.

A lengthy work, and yet the group was so
astounded, overwhelmed by what did flow,
the power of the words the Báb did show,
that everyone along with host did stand,
then knelt before the Báb in homage, and
each kiss'd the hem of robe He wore unplanned.

Then one divine did testify to all
the reasons why he was himself enthralled:
that unique words which from the pen had streamed
were peerless – and beyond this, more it seemed,
that to be able to reveal such lines
so legible and in so short a time
in verses of a number that's so great
(one-third of Qur'án's length it does equate) –
achievement that no mortal can perform
without God's intervention could be born.

Throughout the town the Báb's fame, it did teem.
From every quarter visitors did stream
to understand more deeply what He taught,
or remedy for suffering they sought,
or merely curiosity they brought.

Now Manúchihr the Governor does hear
as these events around the Báb appear.

The Governor decides that he should pay
a visit to the Báb with no delay.

When he arrives for his first visit, there
already present is a group quite rare:
most learned famous of divines around,
in presence of the Báb they all are found.

The Governor had asked these same divines –
had asked them all before, e'en sev'ral times –
to somehow try convincing him of truth
of mission of Muhammad. But forsooth
a satisfact'ry answer never came.
Now to the Báb requests the Gov'nor same.

The Báb replies without delay'r defer,
says: "to your question, which do you prefer:
a verbal or a written answer?" Then
the Gov'nor says, "a written reply – then
both present pleased and future edified."
At once the Báb, His pen on paper glides.

Two ho-ur's time gives fifty pages' sum
to explicate the nature of Islám –
its origin, its character, as well
pervasive influence the pages tell.

The Governor's affected by this course –
sound reasoning and stimulating force,
the detail accurate, with vig'rous style
that charact'rize the verses as they file.

Remaining doubts the Gov'nor's had so long
were all removed by treatise written strong.

So joyfully the Gov'nor says: "Hear me!
For never till today, the heart in me
has ever been convinced of Islám's truth.
Thanks to this exposition, I forsooth
can now declare myself believer firm
in God's Apostle; this I now affirm.
I also testify to my belief
in Source Divine these verses and motif.
No sum of learning has this pow'r allowed;
with superhuman pow'r this Youth's endowed."

The fame spread through the city and beyond.
With jealousy did some hearts now respond.

Particularly, some divines are pained
about the high respect the Báb has gained,
and influence He'll presently exert
on their disciples. They wish to avert.

Back in the Capital, the Grand Vazir
a meeting 'twixt the Báb and Shah does fear.

For Shah might be enamored with the Báb,
embrace His teachings, ruin Vazir's job.

Afraid that Manúchihr will this arrange
and end his own career, his life derange –
alarméd by reports from Isfáhán –
does Haji Mirza Aqasi now spawn
a plan to turn the tide the other way,
and keep the impact of the Báb at bay:
he writes the Chief Mullá in scolding tones,
who then decreases visits to his home;
he writes to other Isfáhán divines
about the Báb, by Whom they feel outshined,
to foster opposition now therein;
from pulpit to denounce Him, one begins.

So Gov'nor holds a meeting in his house,
the flames of animosity to douse –
the Báb, the Chief Mullá, the clergy great,
some absent fearing loss of a debate.

All others there the Báb were questioning,
while He polite and clear was answering.
Then some divines seek idle argument,
so Governor adjourns the whole event.

Protecting peace from vi'lence overthrown,
the Gov'nor keeps the Báb in his own home,
and hosting Him so graciously for weeks
till conclave of the 'Ulamá then speaks.

For heresy, death sentence is declared –
divines and notables who had been scared
gave signature – 'twas seventy in all,
while two of them would not endorse this call.

The Chief Mullá was one who could not hate,
and yet he also did equivocate.
In his own note, objects to punishment –
bears witness to the Báb's accomplishment
as loyal, pious and a siyyid too;
but then advances that if someone who
persistently does voice outrageous claim,
and of mater'al things does show disdain,
conclusion Chief Mullá cannot avoid:
the Báb of reasoned judgment is devoid.

Despite objections, sentence ratified.
To take control, the Gov'nor does decide
t'avert the execution with a plan:
with feint-and-switch, protect the Báb he can.

With thousands of the citizens to see,
five hundred horseman escort openly
to take the Báb and exit Isfáhán
toward the royal presence in Tihrán.

Then secretly, attrition of the guard,
till final ten in Gov'nor's high regard
do quietly return to Gov'nor's place –
clandestinely return the Báb, no trace.

for several months, in utmost secrecy,
in Gov'nor's own apartments do we see
the Báb is safely quartered; and beyond –
by Governor himself is waited on.

A few Bábís allowed to come and see –
get info and instructions happily
to dissipate the rumors they've believed,
and Isfáhání Bábís told to leave.

As sev'ral safe and secret months move on,
a transformation for Manúchihr Khán:
the Revelation of the Báb does he
now fully recognize; he wants to be
of service, with his full wealth consecrate
to help advance the Bábí Cause so great.

Repenting for the way his means were earned,
give to the Báb all of his wealth he yearned.

The Báb accepts his penitence, but He
declines the offered fortune, not to be.

71

The Gov'nor does his other wish relate
to go and meet the Shah, himself update –
persuade the King the Teachings to embrace
and then promote them wide through Persian space;
he also wants to say to King's own ear
of profligacy of the Grand Vazir
as well his folly, help the Shah to see
to discharge Haji Mirza Aqasi.

And finally the Governor confides
his own wish for promoting far and wide
the Teachings of the Báb beyond Írán –
the cherished yearning of Manúchihr Khán.

The Báb with loving graciousness accepts
the Governor's allegiance, and respects
his lofty aspirations, then replies:
"Our days are numbered;" then He specifies –
in three months and nine days, Manúchihr will
succumb to death, immortal glory fill.

The Báb explains that not by Gov'nor's way
will Bábí Cause survive and have its day,
but rather through the poor and lowly's stead,
and sadly also following bloodshed,
the Cause preserve and will consolidate
till soon its fruiting on that Day so great.

The Governor does marvel and rejoice,
and spends his final days on noble choice:
he settles his affairs, and from the Source
grows deeper in the Revelation's force.

Precisely when foretold, he passed away.
From final sets of deeds, the world can say:
through hist'ry's eyes, a glory for Írán
was noble governor – Manúchihr Khán.

When Gov'nor dies, the nephew does succeed –
compared to Manúchihr, a diff'rent breed.
But honoring his uncle, this one writes
to Shah the Báb's location. The King writes:
the Báb must quickly leave from Isfáhán,
come secretly and forthwith to Tihrán.

𝔑ow orders issued from the Shah 'f Írán:
escort the Báb due northwest to Tihrán.
Chief Courier's the only one to know
identity of Prisoner. They go.
Not even escort soldiers are aware
of Who it is they guard or why they care.

An order also strictly from the Crown:
the Pris'ner's not to enter any town.

Late winter 1847 drawn,
proceed they do until they reach Káshán.

At city gate – a stranger, who does wear
his finest clothes, just standing waiting there.

When escort reaches gate, the Báb does say
to stranger there: "Tomorrow's Naw-Rúz Day,"
and "We shall celebrate it in your home;
We are to be your Guest for three nights' own."

This stranger whom the Báb had never met:
a Bábí taught by Mullá Husayn – yet
last night dreamed of the Báb at city gate,
woke up and dressed and prepped and there did wait.
And when the Báb did speak the very words
that in his dream exactly he had heard,

he kiss'd the stirrups of the Báb onsite.
The Courier beheld this wondrous sight,
allow'd the Báb to stay there for three nights,
the interdiction of the king despite.

And as the escort further does advance,
the hearts of all its soldiers are entranced
full by the Báb's compelling dignity,
alluring charm and kindness lovingly,
but still don't know His true identity.

The Courier's devotion is complete –
to serve and please the Báb, his only treat;
he'd even let Him go, would He retreat.

As town of Qum the escort does approach,
the option to go in the soldiers broach.
The royal interdiction they'd defy
and let Him go – His will they shall comply.
They offer for the Báb to visit shrine.
But lovingly the Báb, He does decline;
He tells them that the true believer's heart
has been the Throne of God right from the start,
and He Who now is with them journeying
is Citadel Secure of God the King;
He says He does prefer the country way
instead of ent'ring Qum, so that He may
avoid unholy city on that day.

A kindly gracious welcome, nearby town.
And then the desert roadways, two days down,
are inhospitable, cloudless and hot
and nights are frigid; friendly it is not.

Then from Tihrán not thirty miles away,
a letter from the Grand Vazir to stay.

Afraid is Haji Mirza Aqasi,
resolved to stop the Shah the Báb to see,
does redirect the escort to Kulayn –
outskirting village, a delay to gain.

So tents are pitched in orchard on a hill
where all is peaceful, verdant and so still –
except the murm'ring streams. Allows a time
for rest and solace to the Báb, this clime.

For journey's long and sometimes perilous,
from fam'ly separated, arduous –
fatigued and sad sometimes the Báb would be.
At times they saw Him weeping bitterly,
such that it moved the hearts of soldiery.

But now, what had obstruction been designed
becomes a welcome respite they're assigned.

For Tihrán Bábís, news the Báb is near.
Some come to visit, mutual good cheer.
A few days later, something happens dear:
a letter sealed, a few small gifts we see
come for the Báb; they're from Husayn-Alí !

All see the Báb – His gloom and sorrow lift –
grief changed to praise and thanks for wondrous gift
of correspondence with Husayn-Alí.
Companions marveled at what they did see –
light radiant shone from the Báb brightly.
This comfort, exultation, joy and strength
would Him sustain for many months in length.

A few nights later, hooves are galloping
as for the Báb all frantic are searching;
His tent is empty, soldiers fear escape.
But Courier then does their thought reshape:
"for do not worry – His nobility,
indeed His unbound magnanimity
would ne'er embarrass us for His own sake;
He likely went a private commune take;
He will return, He will not us desert."
With such assurances he did assert.
To reassure his nervous soldiery,
proceeds along the road to Tihrán he...

... and soon does see the Báb now coming near
from d'rection of Tihrán in goodly cheer.

"Did you believe Me to've escaped?" says He.
Chief Courier is deeply moved; we see
he flings himself at Pris'ner's feet, distraught:
"Far be't from me to entertain such thought."

The count'nance of the Báb, now all do see
does shine with radiance and majesty.

And all are awed by pow'r surrounding there –
a reverence profound does fill the air
as calmly He returns to tent, no care.

Three weeks' encampment in the village, rest.
The Báb does write the King to make request
for audience and meeting to occur.
The Grand Vazir, his fear it does recur
of losing his position – power gone
if teachings of the Báb do carry on.

So Haji Mirza Aqasi does play
on worries of unrest on king that prey;
the royal caravan must go away,
defer the Báb until return one day;
till then, the Báb in Ádhirbáyján wait –
suggested by the Grand Vazir this fate.

So ordered by the Shah, and then wrote he
a letter to the Báb of this decree.

Extreme northwest is Ádhirbáyján found
– the corner of Írán, forbidding ground,
with mostly mountain ranges hard and high,
where summit peaks and clefts and gorges lie,
with fertile river valleys hidden nigh.

Already distance traveled from His home
is only halfway to their final zone.

The orders to the Courier were these:
the Báb is to be taken to Tabríz,
no town or city stop along the way,
some money to the Báb the Crown will pay.

The Báb Himself, supports Himself for sure,
and gives the royal stipend to the poor.

When passing by Qazvín the Báb does write –
at first to Grand Vazir in scolding light;
and then to the divines of nearby ville,
Qurratu'l-'Ayn's home city hears His will.

And then the Shaykhí leader of Qazvín
receives a letter too, in verses keen:
"I am the Promised One," the Báb makes plain,
"alluded to by Siyyid Kázim fain."

A few Bábís to rescue Him they try,
convince the Báb to come away they ply.
The Báb declines. "The mountains," He explains,
"of Ádhirbáyján also have their claims."

Indeed with many chances to go free,
He shows He freely chooses not to flee.

In fact, one day while escort nears Tabríz,
on His lean mount He gallops off with ease.
The guards amazed this horse could go so fast;
ahead so swift, they can't catch up at last.
This sprinting did occur a-many day:
the soldiers tire, in saddles could not stay;
while straight as arrow no fatigue He rode
for ho-urs, barely changing posture strode;
and always meeting up again on road.

Becomes a Bábí, Courier betides;
"I should have served You better," he confides.
The Báb, with love, says "you are of My fold;
by Bábís will your conduct be extolled,
your name exalted, bless'd and glorified
eternally" – a source of Bábí pride.

The escort now does Tabríz near attain,
then all the guards do blessing seek to gain:
implore the Báb and humble selves as well,
they kiss His feet and all do bid farewell.

Then nearing Tabríz, custody moves on
to Crown Prince, Gov'nor of Ádhirbáyján.

Tabriz – a proud and bustling city-town.
But many quakes with buildings fallen down,
and scarce are water, fountain, garden, shade.
Still, active city had the people made.

As escort now approaches to the town,
the spreading news within and all around.

The Bábís come – the Báb they try to see.
But strict new guards, they will not let it be.

To see His entry through the city gate
did gather local crowd of number great.
Approaching news – an uproar it creates.
The crier warns that punishment awaits
for those who try to see the Báb, their fates.
But threats do not deter the eager mass,
as thousands wait and watch the entry pass –
some curious, some seeking to know more,
while Bábís kiss the dust His footsteps bore.

Through crowded street to designated house.
Restriction rule: no access to the house.
And yet the guards do acquiesce when He
requests or does invite Bábís to see.
The Báb explains this inconsistency:
the guards are destined by Him and provide
to buffer multitudes, but let inside

the ones whom He desires to meet; attain
His Presence guards are pow'rless to restrain.

The Báb repeats a foresight now foregone –
what He predicted while in Isfáhán:
at least nine months is He to be confined
within the "Open Mountain;" then they'll find
a transfer to the "Grievous Mountain" site.
And five days later prove that He was right:

The isolated mountains ordered to;
a transfer to the Castle of Máh-Kú

As escort goes from Tabríz to Máh-Kú –
Araxes River near and harsh land through –
pass des'late plain, volcanic black outcrops,
through parlous mountain pass with twisted rocks.
At birthplace of the Grand Vazir they do
thus finally arrive at town Máh-Kú.

On hillside steep of mountain sits the town.
At top of hill is castle looking down.
The mountain rises more, above the rook;
a massive overhang above, can't look.
From rocks below the castle gush a stream.
The treach'rous path of entry does careen.
Four towers in the castle, solid, strong.
With summer swelter, winter's chill is long.

A dangerously situated place –
remote and inhospitable, no grace.

As his hometown, the influence we see
enjoyed by Haji Mirza Aqasi.
The people with obed'ent loyalty
are Kurdish Sunnís who the Shí'ihs hate,
especially the Siyyids they berate.

The Grand Vazir thought Bábís won't go there,
and this would isolate the Báb from care –
His influence would decrease everywhere.

And so the order comes from Grand Vazir:
no visitors and strict confinement clear.
Just two companions from Tabríz are near.

Now Alí Khán – the prison governor –
a rough and simple man who does defer
to Haji Mirza Aqasi. To please,
to follow orders: this is all he sees.

And so the Báb's confined within the walls.
The gloom is thick in cell and in the halls.
No light, not even candle breaks the dark
of doorless mud-walled cell, His dwelling stark.
Two guards, four dogs are only other life
within the castle – desolation rife.

But soon the Prisn'er's influence is felt
by castle guards with whom He daily dealt.

From moment of arrival, they do see
extr'ordinary character has He.
His wisdom, tender love and gentle charm
affect the guards, whose hearts begin to warm.
And then the guards tell people in the town;
attraction to the Báb spreads all around.

The peasant farmers, 'neath the castle they
now gather, catch a glimpse of Him each day
and ask for blessing of their work today;
or settle quarrels, there invoke His name
to tell the truth, resolve dispute their aim.

Between the town and castle for supplies,
the Báb's companion secretary tries –
pass messages as well, both up and down
between the Báb and Bábís there in town
who did indeed complete the trek, and yet
arrive then barred from seeing Him, regret.

This problem, though, it seems may soon be gone:
the Báb says He will soon ask Alí Khán
to change his attitude and policies
toward the gathered visiting Bábís.

Next morning frantic knocks at castle gate;
they come from Alí Khán in altered state:
submissive at the threshold, humble face,
in wonder, begs to come upon the place
where he may enter Pris'ner's Presence now –
in trembling agitation, rev'rent bow,
and flinging self at Pris'ner's feet, says he:
"Deliver me from my perplexity!"
And then he narrates what had come to be:

While riding in the wilderness at dawn,
approaching gates of town this morning gone,
did he behold the Báb at riverside
engaged in off'ring prayer, glorified.

So Alí Khán awaited to approach
for unpermitted outing to reproach.

The Báb was wrapt in worship – totally,
and of Himself forgetful utterly.

When Alí Khán approaching did begin –
and saw the rapt'rous state the Báb was in
and wholly unaware of all that's near –
was Alí Khán gripped sudden with great fear,
and recoil'd at the thought that he may be
disturbing of the Báb's high ecstasy.

Instead did Alí Khán decide to leave
and go rebuke the guards for that reprieve.

But at the castle, evidence disclosed:
both outer gate and inner were still closed.
So either there's no chance the Báb's inside,
or there's no way He ever came outside.
Yet clearly was He just outside no doubt,
while also none can contradict about
the fact that Alí Khán does now see clear
with wonder that the Báb is seated here
before him in the prison cell! But how?
"I'm utterly confounded! Help me now!"

The Báb explains with loving confidence
the how and why of this co-incidence:

"What you have witnessed – undeni'ble, true.
This Revelation and its Author too
have you belittled and disdained till now.
But God does spare you punishment somehow,
and willed He to reveal t'your eyes the Truth.
Interposition His has now forsooth
instilled the love into your open heart
for His own Chosen One, and helped you start
to recognize, e'en at this very hour,
His true Faith's unconquerable power."

At once does Alí Khán beseech that he
may by the Báb henceforth forgiven be,
and may be given opportunity
to wash away his stain of cru-el-ty.

To start, he begs the Báb to bring within
a Bábí in town waiting to see Him –
who's waited there for weeks but was denied,
along with many others who have tried.

Then Alí Khán devoted does become.
Gates open daytime, visitors can come.

Does all he can to mitigate the jail
as from his eyes asunder torn the veil.

Sends gifts of fruit, and ev'ry Friday he
pays visit to the Báb personally.

And over time devotion even more
to serve new Master's wish more than before.

The spies of Haji Mirza Aqasi
report on weeks of this activity.
The Grand Vazir is furious, enraged –
bewildered that the Dove sings from His cage.
For all of his attempt to isolate,
the opposite effect it does equate,
the circumstances do his plan frustrate.
Instead of Teachings and the Báb put down,
they've now been introduced to his hometown.

From everywhere in Persia, Bábís come
for pilgrimage of three days – 'tis their sum
to visit with their Master and receive
instructions for their teaching, then they leave.

Indeed the castle isolation gave
some peace that guaranteed the Báb a wave
of steady revelation of His Word –
to formulate His Teachings undeterred,
record it all, instruct the Bábís, and
disseminate it all throughout the land.
Beyond the lines of Persia they expand.

𝖂𝖍𝖎𝖑𝖊 nine months in Máh-Kú, there were reveal'd
so many Writings – storehouse was unseal'd.
Five hundred thousand verses prior to;
exceeded was that number in Máh-Kú.

The Báb does dictate, taken down by scribe –
His voice is heard at foot of mount, outside.
The melody of chanting, rhythmic flow
of verses streaming from His lips, bestow
a mountain-valley echo down below.

By teachings, principles and utt'rance art
is penetrating soul, vibrating heart.

Within that span of time, the Báb did write
upon a varied range of topics bright.

Nine commentaries fresh on the Qur'án.
To clergy in each city of Írán,
and to those in Najaf and Karbilá.
As well, communications to the Shah.

And also came the "Seven Proofs" – a Book –
a measure of God's Word for those who look;
both Arabic and Persian did He write
of Seven Proofs for either kind of sight.

He also wrote the Arabic Bayán,
and started on the Persian-writ Bayán.

Eight thousand verses Persian Bayán holds.
The core of Bábí teaching it unfolds –
with theologic explanation wide,
and many terms and ideas clarified,
progression of the Prophets does He frame,
and Cycle of Religion does explain,
and He is next – a Cycle new proclaims;
with His own Prophethood, He abrogates
a legion of Muhammad's laws, abates;
new Laws He does reveal for this new Age;
but also warns: 'twill be a fleeting stage.

For everything revolves around the One
Who not so long from now is yet to come.
Indeed "Him Whom God Shall Make Manifest" –
of everyone, the Báb does love Him best.
The Báb Himself but serves at His command,
is but a ring on Finger of His Hand.

For Promised One the Bayán's full of praise
and of anticipation of His days.
With countless ref'rences for all to purge
their vision and to watch, the Book does urge.
The Promised One will suddenly shine bright.
A nineteen yearly respite does it cite.

Today's disciples, many will attain
the Presence of that Promised One, and gain
admittance to His most frequented Fane.

The Promised One will keep or will reject
whatever from the Bayán He'll elect.

His suffering, it certainly will be
moreso than other Prophets' history.

Explicit when the Bayán it relays:

"Well is it with him who fixeth his gaze
upon the order of Bahá'u'lláh."

And thus the Báb relates what He foresaw.

The winter's cold in castle and in town.
A constant stream of pilgrims and renown.

While civil unrest elsewhere in Írán.
The local leaders, province Khurásán,
rebel against the cap'tal in Tihrán.

Mullá Husayn is right there in Mashhad,
avoiding civil situation bad.

Decides to walk to Máh-Kú all the way –
nine-hundred miles on foot his chosen way.
Through villages and towns along his route,
the Bábís greet him, eagerly salute.
They offer help but he declines with grace;
his ardent faith, completely steadfast pace
the hearts of all he meets inspire and brace.

While in Tihrán, a special gift gets he:
a secret meeting with Husayn-Alí!

In winter 1848 he's on
the northward trek toward Ádhirbáyján.

Then eve of Naw-Rúz, one day from Máh-Kú,
a mystic moment preps the way anew.

That night does Alí Khán now have a dream:
Muhammad as God's Prophet there does seem
to be arriving at Máh-Kú with friend,
and Alí Khán runs out there to attend.
At bridge he starts to kiss the Prophet's cloak,
and this is point in dream when he awoke.

So Alí Khán gets ready, goes to stream,
and there beholds the two men from his dream.
It's Mullá Husayn and his company.
Then Alí Khán does prostrate joyfully,
escorts the travelers so they may see
the Báb, Who waits inside the gate calmly.

A loving welcome at the very least.
In Pris'ner's room they have the Naw-Rúz feast.

First time permitted: an in-castle stay;
Mullá Husayn's at Máh-Kú for nine days.

By this time has the Bábí Movement grown
across Írán from teaching and renown
of Living Letters, plus activity
of other Bábís who teach eagerly –
so much that a cascading growth occurs
of tens of thousands, over Persia stirs.

Important things the Báb does have to say
to Mullá Husayn during his brief stay:
predicts a transfer soon to somewhere else –
another mountain, tell nobody else.

"You're leaving soon," He tells Mullá Husayn.
"Of Bábís, fortify faith, hearts inflame.
To Tabríz, Zanján, Qazvín and Tihrán,
then make your way, go to Mázindarán.
Performance of great deeds you will be cast,
to dwarf the feats a-mighty from the past.
Both strength and guidance will descend on you
to reinforce the things you're yet to do.
Your days of horsemanship are yet to come.
You're destined to exhibit in a sum
such courage, skill and heroism bold
eclipsing greatest deeds of heroes old."

The spies of Haji Mirza Aqasi
of Alí Khán and pilgrims do they see,
reporting all of it to Grand Vazir,
who in a new direction wants to steer.

A quick command to Pris'ner move gives he –
away to Chihríq, immediately .

To Grievous Mountain –

Chihríq is its name –
near Zoroaster's birthplace, region's fame.
Location desolate. A fortress grim
at foot of cliff-rock steep, there standing dim.

Arriving April 1848.
A barren nowhere recapitulates:
another fail'd confinement now awaits.

The warden of the prison – Yahyá Khán -
harsh Kurdish chieftain from Ádhirbáyján,
with orders like his peer at Máh-Kú, vowed
confinement strict, no visitors allowed.

But once again, not long in Pris'ner's stay,
his orders he's unable to obey.
The Pris'ner's love does his heart penetrate,
as well his being it does captivate.

And soon does warden for all access grant.
The swell of visitors the small town can't
accommodate, so overflow does stay
at 'nother town about an hour away.

The local Kurds hate Shí'ihs even more
than locals of Máh-Kú had done before.

But once again is hate turned into love,
devotion for the Pris'ner kept above.
At daybreak, blessing sought for daily care;
at eve, of Holy Pris'ner stories share.

From nearby town the locals come to see,
and soon a number do become Bábí.

Religious teachers, ruling officers –
among the Báb's avowéd followers.

One government official do we see –
a learned fluent man, renowned is he –
opposed the Báb vituperatingly.
Then has a dream, then to the Báb he writes;
the Báb replies, then to the prison site
the man he goes, His Presence to attain;
his full acceptance of the Báb is fain;
he then begins to teach most eagerly,
he also writes a treatise earnestly,
establishing the Báb's validity.
"Dayyán" is his new name, identity.

One day a dervish to the town arrives –
walked all the way from India, survives
barefoot, poor clothes, with only staff and bowl.
Had been a rich navváb, then in his soul
a vision of the Báb he has one day:
the Báb does gaze and steal his heart away.
The dream directs and summons to Írán,
"Divest yourself, come to Ádhirbáyján."
Arriving, he attains his heart's desire
in Presence of the Báb, and then aspire.
Instructions to return to whence he came,
and teach where he shall go and spread His Name.
The dervish then sets out, his mission clear.
Alone he goes, from hist'ry disappear.

The spies nearby do watch and do report
on all they learn of to the royal court.
And father of Dayyán we then do see –
a friend of Haji Mirza Aqasi –
does write a full report to Grand Vazir,
exacerbating his inherent fear.
Another climacteric drawing near;
his own position now in jeopardy
as Shah is dying, everyone does see.

And meanwhile

elsewhere 'cross the country do
the Letters of the Living continue
to teach – now prep the people with no rest
for "Him Whom God" will soon "Make Manifest."

When Mullá Husayn left Ádhirbáyján,
he taught the towns instructed till Tihrán,
where visit he had with Husayn-Alí
before embarking on his odyssey.

To Mázindarán then he made his way,
where fertile soil and farm and hamlet lay.

A promise from the Báb does come to mind:
therein a "hidden treasure" he would find.

In Bárfurúsh he stops and there he meets
Quddús, who's there in his hometown and greets.

Since exiled from Shíráz, Quddús had been
in motion, travel teaching, and did win
achievements for the Bábí Cause; it grows;
returning home to Bárfurúsh he goes.

Now Quddús, he does host Mullá Husayn
while catching up, in deepest friendship gain.

One time, Quddús a manuscript does show.
And when he reads does Mullá Husayn know
the power there within the words he read –
so startled is he, shaken when he said
the author of these words in-spi-red by
a Fount beyond men's learning, can't deny;
sublimity of all these words is real,
and he accepts the truth that they reveal.

Quddús's silent affect follows then.
Husayn discerns: it was Quddús's pen
that wrote the treatise. And so this is when
Husayn does reverently rise and bow,
and voice perceptions visiting him now:

"The hidden treasure of the Báb now lies
as He had said – unveil'd before my eyes.
Though prison'd up in fort my Master be,
His sign is manifest here before me.
And here in Mázindarán have I found
reflection of His glory does abound."

From that time forward Mullá Husayn shows
to Quddús humble def'rence, and he goes
to instantly, whatever Quddús asks,
enact them as his most important tasks.

At Quddús's instructions does Husayn
to Mashhad go. And there he does arrange
to purchase property, then use the place –
construction of a house to serve as base
of teaching work for Quddús and Husayn –
and "Bábíyyih" will be the place's name.
When Quddús joins, and when the building's done,
a wave of teaching actively begun
throughout Mashhad and province Khurásán.

The Bábís see in Quddús virtues of
his honor, insight, leadership and love,
his piety and understanding too –
and Bábís' spirit galvanize, renew.

𝔄𝔪𝔬𝔫𝔤 the Persian Bábís circulates
a letter from the Báb – disseminates.
An unknown purpose has He in His sights,
when "hasten to the land of Khá" He writes.

So on to Khurásán some Bábís head.
Some also go from Karbilá; they're led
by none else but Qurratu'l-'Ayn we see,
who in Iráq's been teaching steadily
with passion, courage, insight, eloquence –
that Muslim skeptics oft she does convince,
infuriating many fam'ly men
and clergy in and out of clan and ken.

Among Bábís she's also blazing trail.
Superlative her mind – it cannot fail
to fellow Bábís' hearts excite, inspire;
while more traditioned ones, arouse their ire.

She openly advances with no qualm
the Bábí Faith is sep'rate from Islám.
And citing verses from the Báb's Bayán
to abrogate what's found in the Qur'án:
discard old laws, for new ones now exist,
abandon old tradition, now insist
on patterns new – a novel life and age.

And many Bábís take this to be sage,
while others do oppose with fear or rage.

This independence – stirrings have begun:
a dialectic happening with some,
preamble of a larger change to come.

When summons of the Báb does reach her hand,
Qurratu'l-'Ayn Iráq's departing, and
to Khurásán begins to make her way.
In hometown of Qazvín, a respite stay.

From her arrival in Qazvín occur
reactions from the clan, and clergy stir –
involving Bábís too, both wise and fool,
and escalating on toward misrule.
Attacks and death on both sides of the duel.

Qurratu'l-'Ayn, though not directly part,
is house-arrested, she is kept apart.

But as her life to peril it does change,
Husayn-Alí a rescue does arrange,
and swiftly to Tihrán is taken she –
the guest of honor of Husayn-Alí.

While in Tihrán, Qurratu'l-'Ayn does see
supernal greatness of Husayn-Alí.
Expressing this discernment soon she'll be,
in odes of hers that soon will written be.

Then after rest and visit in Tihrán,
Qurratu'l-'Ayn does go to Khurásán.

And meanwhile over in Mashhad we see
a surge of teaching and activity
led on by Quddús and Mullá Husayn.
The Bábíyyih does many visits gain.

In wake of civil discord recently,
authorities are skittish; we can see
they misconstrue the Bábís with alarm.
Attack and death, on both sides there is harm.
The uproar it does threaten to consume,
so Mullá Husayn dissipates the loom:
a peaceful way he clearly advocates,
accepting martyrdom he even states,
alluding that his own in future waits.

Prince Hamzih Mirza – government command –
an order does he issue from his stand
and summons Mullá Husayn to his place;
a camp in city outskirts is his base.

As Mullá Husayn summons does obey,
Quddús joins other Bábís on their way,
converging in the hamlet of Badasht.
But Mullá Husayn's aspirations dashed
as prince commander now does him detain
while Quddús meets up with Qurratu'l-'Ayn.

Of all the Bábís there, most glad to see:
Badasht is favored by Husayn-Alí.

At Badasht – Bábís number eighty-one,
disciples learned, days of twenty-one.

And they are all guests of Husayn-Alí.
Significance unknown to all but three.

Though Bayán many laws did abrogate,
still many Bábís did equivocate.
Though recognize the Báb, they still observe
traditions of the past – they do preserve –
preventing recognition full and true:
from Islám sep'rate, Dispensation new.

Yet others understand, and eager they
to follow the new laws of the new Day.

And permeating this dichotomy –
a growing tension in community.

Husayn-Alí, Quddús, Qurratu'l-'Ayn
together guide the gathering to gain
the Bábís' recognition of the claim:
an offshoot or an independent Name?

The three of them decide it is the time
to now resolve the question for all time,
and demonstrate the Báb had brought a true
and independent Revelation new.

Three gardens had been rented for those days –
a tent on each, where everybody stays.
The three great friends, who did all oversee,
were each a host at one tent of the three.

A consultation earnest, steadily
addressing matters, ideas, inquiry.

Among the time that Bábís do converse,
each day Husayn-Alí revealing verse
that's chanted then to all without rehearse.

Each day, the abrogation of a law,
repudiating a tradition saw.

Husayn-Alí gives each one a new name.
Then letters from the Báb which use the same
to each participant arriving soon –
confirming name bestowals, all in tune.

Among them:
                   when Quddús received his name;

   and "Táhirih" replaced "Qurratu'l-'Ayn;"

      "Bahá" the title for Husayn-Alí –
      "Bahá'u'lláh": His name to history.

Amidst the argument and the debate,
the diff'rent viewpoints each repudiate.

The polarizing forms begin to make
"preserve tradition" versus "sep'rate, break."

Quddús would verbalize tradition's view
while Táhirih would the opposing view,
and soon they each did represent a side
to one of which all had identified.

Quddús and Táhirih had planned ahead
delib'rately to stoke this growing dread,
and each would don their designated role
to walk the Bábís t'ward the final goal.

Quddús and Táhirih don't really fight –
but outwardly a show to shed the light,
evoke and then externalize viewpoints
that everyone internally appoints –
opposing till it reaches crisis point.
Delib'rately they nurture with their sight
emerging pol'rization to this height.

Behind their percolating shock and awe –
the quiet guidance of Bahá'u'lláh.

No one suspects the two antagonists
are actually both protagonists
of single process, guided so unique
all by Bahá'u'lláh toward its peak.

The climax will a confrontation be,
arranged to force the harsh dichotomy –
to break the bonds of old and then forsooth
resolve the crisis and unveil the Truth.

One day Bahá'u'lláh was in His tent.
Quddús and other Bábís, there they went.

Assembled there are all Bábís but one –
'tis Táhirih, expects Quddús to come.

Her messenger invites him to her tent.
Quddús refuses, says the ties are rent.

The messenger goes back, returns again,
says Táhirih insists he join her then.

Again Quddús refuses – no redress.
The messenger is caught between – distress.

And in this tableau tense in front of all
does Táhirih appear before them all –
arriving unannounced and suddenly,
adornéd and unveil'd for all to see,
her beauty unconceal'd entrancingly.

Aghast with consternation was the crowd,
that some of them did even cry aloud:
" 'Tis inconceivable that Táhirih,
the new embodiment of Fátimih,
would tear the veil away from her own face –
the purity of woman thus disgrace."

With quiet dignity and bright with joy,
serenity and rad'ance unalloyed –
she enters and she seats herself beside
Bahá'u'lláh and Quddús there inside.

The Bábís' speechless shock, bewilderment
for some become a fear belligerent.

As several flee, one cuts his throat onsite.
Beyond them all, the most alarming sight:

Quddús is holding unsheath'd sword in hand,
suffusing anger on his visage, and
appearing as if any moment he
might strike down Táhirih decisively.

Now this exquisite moment is the one
toward which all the guiding work did come.
The ties are crack'd and ready for the break;
the mind and heart are ready to awake;
and thus a matchless Táhirih, she spake:

"Amid the gardens, rivers, verily
the pious in the seat of truth shall be,
within the Presence of the potent King" –
toward Bahá'u'lláh she is gazing.

"I am the Word the Qá'im is to say –
the Word which shall induce to flee away
the chiefs and noble of the earth that day!"

"Festivity, rejoice – this is the day
the fetters of the past are burst away!"

Thus Táhirih did speak with words to last;
indeed she truly was the Trumpet Blast.

Debate, division bide a few more days –
repudiation of each other's ways,
gainsaying the authority of each –
confusion, tension growing out of reach.

Quddús and Táhirih do drive the squall
by plan, Bahá'u'lláh behind it all.

There hovering until the time is right,
and then decisively restoring sight –
Bahá'u'lláh does intervene so clear
with loving wisdom, bringing spirits near:
a reconciliation 'twixt the two,
and clarify the Bábí point of view,
direct it to constructive action too.

The show of conflict led the Bábís to,
Bahá'u'lláh sublimely leads them through.

With greater strength, proclaiming a new day,
traditions from Islám do fall away.

Unfortunately, remnants of the past
do take some more deflection to be cast.

Some do misuse the "break" to justify
a lack of moral discipline, and try
some mischievous behavior that provokes
retaliate attack from local folks.

And during months that follow the event,
complaining letters to the Báb are sent
about the things that Táhirih did say.
The Báb supports her, silencing the fray.
The Báb does to these questions thus refer
with: "What am I to say regarding her
whom Tongue of Power 'Táhirih' did name?" –
thus silencing attempts to her defame.

Faint-hearted of the Bábís fall away.
Remaining – greatly altered from that day:
while shedding their Islám identity,
asserting independence as Bábí.

Departing from Badasht with their new pact,
from Níyálá the Bábís were attack'd.
They all dispersed except a very few
remaining with Bahá'u'lláh – He Who
did calm the onslaught of attackers, and
retrieved the pinch'd possessions from the band.

Reconstituted Bábís better off:
the troublous ones recanted and took off;
a purged and strengthened group had cleared the way
to now proclaim new laws of a new Day.

And most of them to Mázindarán go.
Among them, Táhirih – her verses flow
in odes reverberating in the hills
that magnify the Báb, and further still
they praise Bahá'u'lláh for things fulfilled.

To home in Núr, Bahá'u'lláh proceeds.
Quddús's plan diverted and recedes
as he is stopped and placed on house arrest
by local mujtahid's unjust request.

Now Táhirih was also soon to be
arrested by nearby authority.
At first detained there in Mázindarán,
and later was she transferred to Tihrán.

Someone successfully convinced the king:
Bahá'u'lláh had caused an uprising.

The Shah determines that Husayn-Alí
is to be put to death summarily.

The king commands a local son of friend:
arrest Husayn-Alí, to Tihrán send.

The son, devoted to Husayn-Alí –
distressed by what is now about to be –
does not divulge the news to anyone.
Bahá'u'lláh discerneth in the son
his sorrow, and then with the eye of God
advises him to put his trust in God.

The next day as the two of them did walk,
a horseman messenger with son did talk;
his heart relieved, released from any dread,
he tells Bahá'u'lláh: "The Shah is dead."
Then showing royal summons, they do see
the document now has no eff'cacy.

That night the two did spend in company –
glad atmosphere of calm security.

Now during this whole time, Mullá Husayn
by Prince Commander Hamzih was detained.

Then when he was released, on to Mashhad.
Preparing an excursion been he had
when messenger from Chihríq did appear –
a message and green turban was brought here.
The Báb did send instructions to him clear:

"Adorn your head with My green turban do.
With the Black Standard unfurl'd before you,
to My Quddús lend your help, hasten do."

So Mullá Husayn now will do his best
to rescue Quddús from his house arrest.
Assembling some companions does he do.
With him are numbers of two-hundred-two.

July of 1848 do they
set out across the countryside away –
green turban there on Mullá Husayn's head,
Black Standard at the fore, they thus were led.

With no coincidence it does invoke
millennial Hadíth that had been spoke:
"If Standard Black from Khurásán proceeds,
should ye behold, then hasten in your deeds
toward them, inasmuch as they proclaim
the Promised Mihdí's advent and His Name."

Through villages and towns along the way –
proclaim the message, blazon the new Day.

Some join the Cause, declare themselves Bábís,
while most of others show hostilities.

While that is going on in Khurásán,
a culmination in Ádhirbáyján.

The Grand Vazir does fear the Shah's demise;
his prison plan, reality defies.
So curry favor in the clergy's eyes:
the Grand Vazir thus orders, to appease,
the Báb is to be taken to Tabríz
wherein there will occur, he does announce,
a clergy convocation to pronounce
about the Báb a judgment, punishment –
with aim to end His growing movément.

Before the summons even had occurred,
the Báb already did put out the word
to Bábís for the area to leave
and all of His new Writings to retrieve –
and put themselves within a place of ease,
and Writings keep at safe place in Tabríz.

Then summons from Vazir arrives one day.
The escort then begins to make its way.

In transit, through a little town they pass.
Prince gov'nor, he wants to the Báb harass.

So when the Báb does to the bath proceed,
the gov'nor offers to the Báb a steed
that's known to be a wild and dangerous one,
and able to control it is no one.
A test of courage of the Báb begun.

The horse groom warns the Báb about the plot.
The Báb serenely says to him: "Fear not.
Do as you have been bidden." Then says He,
"Commit us to the care of th'Almighty."

The people know the plan and come to see –
the public square is crowded, viewing spree.

The Báb approaches new mount quietly,
the bridle takes, caressing soothingly.

The horse completely still when He does mount,
and carries Him serene by all account.

The rushing crowd does follow after Him
to kiss His stirrups, be where He has been.
As guards hold back the crowd, they all do see
the prince on foot does Him accompany;
he walks beside the Báb to bath and back.
The people follow Him as in a pack.
And even water He does use that day –
the crowd does rush to carry it away.

The gov'nor prince's house is daily thronged
by those to see or meet the Pris'ner Wronged.

While there, the Báb in mind of artist dawns –
the only portrait of Him ever drawn.

July of 1848, it sees

– as Mullá Husayn marches with Bábís –
the Báb with escort reaches to Tabríz.

The city is in turmoil as it waits.
The trial at gov'nor's home anticipates.

The gov'nor – young crown prince, heir to the throne –
a witness of the trial, though not full grown.

And as the Báb arrives at gov'nor's place,
the crowds besiege the open entry space.

Guards force a clearing path for Him to go;
arrive at hall, it's fully crowded so.

The stars of clergy ranks can all be seen,
as well the Crown Prince Gov'nor, Nás'ri'd-Dín.

A frivolous procedure is the sport;
it's predetermined for a kang'roo court.

The Báb does enter, everyone He greets,
and then He takes the only vacant seat –
the Prince's seat of honor self-assigns
as majesty and power from Him shines.

As dignity does from His Being flow,
mysteriously silent room does grow.

Some time the nerve to speak does no one show.
Then finally the questioning does go.

"Who do you claim to be?" is firstly sought.
"And say, what is the message you have brought?"

His voice rings strong and clear, and it does stun:

"I am, I am, I am the Promised One!"

He then proceeds to openly proclaim:

"A thousand years ye have invoked My Name,
upon Whose mention do ye all arise,
Whose advent you have longed will fill your eyes,
Whose Revelation you've asked God to speed."

And then He tells them that which all must heed:

"The people of the East and West, they must
obey My word and pledge their troth and trust."

Awestruck the room, the Báb has torn the veil –
heads bowing down and faces growing pale.

Then one perverse and insincere divine
did scold the Báb, insult Him and malign,
accusing that to region He had come
to create turmoil in Ádhirbáyján.
Then simply, calmly does the Báb respond:

"I have not come here of My own accord.
I have been summoned here – a prison ward."

More scolding from the priest, no meanness spared.
The Báb says calmly, claim already aired:

"I maintain what I've already declared."

Some try to quibble academic points –
minutiae they criteria appoint.

The Báb admits He knows not of these themes;
He parries, not engaging with their schemes.

A courteous fair-minded mujtahid
is more respectful with the things he said;
he asked the Báb if there was evidence
that may support His claim of eminence.

The Báb says that God's Word is its own proof –
'twas for Qur'án, 'tis now for His behoof.

"The power to produce such evidence
by God to Me is given – to dispense
such verses in two days and nights, reveal
of such a number and of such appeal
to equal the Qur'án,"

He simply states.
Upon request, no forethought, He creates
a steady stream of verses now and clear –
sublime, divine as all around Him hear.

A rude man interrupts and causes breach –
objection 'bout the grammar of His speech.

The Báb says even Qur'án is not bound
by grammar rules, and in it can be found
irregularities that do abound;
the Word of God is never subject to
the limits of His creatures, thus He too.

The Báb resumes His revelation stream.
More interruption rude becomes their scheme –
hair-splitting grammar or some obscure theme.

The Báb, He will not dignify this scene.

He quotes a passage from the Qur'án free:
"Far be the glory of thy Lord," says He,
"from what they do impute to Him." Then He
does rise and leave the meeting instantly.

A few divines, unhappy how this went –
discourtesy toward the Báb, misspent.

The others, for their own positions fear,
demanding action swift and very clear,
decide on corp'ral punishment that day.
The civil guards refuse to act this way.

So chief of the religious court does beat
the Báb with bastinado on His feet
eleven times, and once it strikes His face –
a wound to add to pain and to disgrace.

Physician British, Dr. Cormick treats
the inj'ries of the Báb. Few times he meets.
In correspondence following his job –
a fav'rable impression of the Báb.
Describes His manner and melod'ous voice,
impressions of His Faith where there is choice,
a non-restraint of women he'll equate,
a non-fanatic Faith he does relate.

Then not long after month of August turns,
to Chihríq prison back the Báb returns.

𝔇𝔢𝔰𝔭𝔦𝔱𝔢 the machinations and the scheme
of Grand Vazir and of the clergy team,
"of all the schemers, God does scheme the best."
The Hand of the Divine did take this test
and turned it 'round to satisfy His end:
a Westerner to Westerner does send
view positive direct encounter from –
preamble of diffusions yet to come.

Beyond this, more important do we see:
the trial designed to crush decisively –
the Báb turned into where He publicly
announced His claim and station openly,
relating its command explicitly.

And what became of those who hurt the Báb?
Rewarded for preserving their own job?

The one who did the bastinado beat –
the chief of clergy court, his death did meet:
soon after did paralysis ensue,
within a year a painful end he knew.

And what of Haji Mirza Aqasi? –
The Antichrist of Rev'lation Bábí ...
At every turn and opportunity,
exerted to extinguish Light to be ...

Upon return to Chihríq prison cell,
the Báb does write a letter that does tell
direct to Grand Vazir the consequence
of Vazir's action t'ward His innocence.

The letter's title – "the Sermon of Wrath;"
it signals what is the unfolding path.

The letter goes to Hujjat, who does see
it gets to Haji Mirza Aqasi.

And by the time the letter has arrived,
the Grand Vazir's career has not survived.
Just prior to the Shah's demise is he
deserted, shunned – with nowhere he can be.

In fear he flees the court, but turned away
from Tihrán and Máh-Kú – nowhere to stay;
his fortune taken when the king does die,
to Karbilá he goes and there does lie.

A year he'll languish there, declining tone –
until he dies – sick, friendless and alone.

As news of the Báb's triumph in Tabríz
spread throughout Persia, galvanized Bábís.
Their zeal and teaching thereby did increase,
as did reaction of their enemies –
especially the brand new Grand Vazir,
increasing persecution far and near.

Young Nás'ri'd-Dín, the new Shah of Írán.
New Grand Vazir is Mirza Taqi Khán.

Unfriendly is the king, just 17.
The Grand Vazir – prime minister – is seen
quite capable, strong willed and iron heart
more than his predecessor from the start;
did hate the Báb, did want to play his part.

In all but name was Mirza Taqi Khán
the ruler now of all throughout Írán.
Determined not to make the same mistake
that Haji Mirza Aqasi did make
by waiting to take action 'bout the Báb,
immediate proactive is his job
to launch a civil and religious charge
against the Bábí movement now so large.

The Báb returns to Chihríq, does resume
His visitors and correspondence soon.

One visitor – His uncle came to be
with Him a while, and happy then was He.

And many, many Writings more reveals.
The purpose of His mission He unseals
as Persian Bayán does He thus complete –
the core of His own Dispensation's seat.

And elsewhere

does the peaceful march proceed –
Black Standard, Mullá Husayn on his steed.

And Bábís from Badasht do join the rest
to rescue Quddús from his house arrest,
as hundreds on the long march ride the quest.

Hostility toward the band does grow –
unable to reside where'er they go.
They've no intention combat or of arms –
just demonstrate belief with no one's harm;
just want to show faith in the Báb do they
by vision share and His new laws obey.

But populace reaction getting strong.
And Mullá Husayn sees it won't be long
before the danger level crosses line
to point of making choices, 'twill be time.

To company, the warning he gives voice –
philosophy and action, make your choice.
Advises Bábí path is sacrifice,
a martyr's destiny is his advice.
Predicts that he and seventy-two more –
this destiny is what will be in store.

And based upon what Mullá Husayn told,
then twenty-one decide to leave the fold;
he tells remaining: set aside the rest
but swords and steeds, to ready for the test.

To order a jihad, tradition told
the Qá'im, Twelfth Imám that power'd hold.

The Báb forbade "the slaying of a soul."

The Bábís of this were not yet aware,
and knew not about what He did declare
regarding vi-o-lence and of warfare.
And due to circumstances growing dire,
they had no way to even thus inquire.

In absence of an order for jihad,
and not aware 'twas now forbade by God –
a middle-zone approach and way they must
then follow, for which old Tradition trust:
be arméd to defend, defend alone;
or if unable to defend is known,
then emulate Imám Husayn, and die
with honesty – upholding true from lie.

Thus did Mullá Husayn now advocate,
as did Quddús at soon and later date:
defend with honor, but attack do not;
no driving home advantage you have got;
and do not strike unnecessary blows –
the noble way in eyes of God, Who knows.

Now as the march near Bárfurúsh does come,
reaction fierce within that town's begun.

Its chief divine is jealous and does hate
in light of changes Quddús did create.
Quddús had taught, and hundreds did convert.
Bloodthirsty is the chief divine to hurt.

Vituperously does he now denounce
the march and leaders, and he does pronounce
jihadi purpose to oppose the band;
does rouse the town to fury rising. And
the whole town rises up and rushes out –
all manner of a weapon wave about –
attacking the Bábís.
                              And even when
they do descend –"do not attack; defend!"

And even when the injuries do come,
says Mullá Husayn: "time is not yet come."

When seven die, the seventh one so meek,
then finally does Mullá Husayn speak –
allowing Bábís to repulse the foe.

And he himself upon his horse does go,
pursuing one who killed the sweet Bábí.

The killer – refuge takes behind a tree,
and holding musket vertic'lly in front –
protects with tree and barrel from affront.

On horse Mullá Husayn sweeps down on foe –
a single mighty stroke of sword let go.

That stroke cuts through the tree, the gun, the man –
bisecting all three full, like no sword can!

This feat astonishing did do the job
to terror strike in hearts of wayward mob.

Words of the Báb beginning to fulfill
of heroism, horsemanship and skill.

The fame of this did spread both far and near,
and even reached the ears of Grand Vazir.

But in that moment, exigency needs
to stop the town's attack with further deeds.

So forcing through the mob's retreating rows,
and heedless of the raining bullets, goes
Mullá Husayn – does head toward the town.
All who attack – with single stroke cut down.

He gallops to the chief divine's own house
wherein the priest does hide as if a mouse.

Mullá Husayn does circle that house thrice,
    then calls out openly with no device,
says:
        "Let that wretched coward who'd incite,
and then conceal himself, now come to sight.
Let him emerge and demonstrate his case.
For we all know that one must show his face,
and by example lead the cause he'll teach,
himself at head of marching force till breach –
especially if holy war he'll preach!"

"Peace! Peace!" the mob does cry – surrender they.

The chief divine does not come out that day.

Then Mullá Husayn, he the mob does shame
for acts they did commit in Prophet's name:

"For *not* did the Apostle ever say
that path of Islám was to treat this way
the unbeliever or the infidel.
Moreover must you know what I now tell:
we Bábís don't repudiate Islám.
So heed this with clear minds and spirits calm."

The mob dispers'd when these words he did ply.
Bábís to local caravanserai.

Now chief divine comes out of house, and then
another mob attack he plans again.

Outside the hostel's gates is gathered mob.
Within, Mullá Husayn conceives a job.
Unknowing what awaits outside the wall,
he asks a volunteer to adhán call –
to raise the call to pra'er can be a balm
to show the town that Bábís love Islám,
and show their friendship and their faithfulness.
A youth does rise with gladsome eagerness,
ascends to height of caravanserai
and does begin the prayer-call to cry.

The op'ning phrase is said, then he's shot down
by someone in the mob below in town.

A second youth ascends, continues call –
and partway through adhán is shot, does fall.

A third does carry on in second's stead,
and he again is shot. All three are dead.

This Bábí act of high fidelity
did demonstrate the town's own perfidy.

Mullá Husayn the gates threw open, and
did lead a charge on steed with sword in hand.

Again the mob in panic, they did flee;
again they begged for peace and clemency.

As Bárfurúshís pleaded for reprieve,
their leaders begg'd Mullá Husayn to leave.
The agitation would thereby decrease
if separation 'twixt the groups increase.

The military chief of province said,
with promise on Qur'án, they would be led
with escort safely through the forest, and
told escort chief to do this – a command.

But then the chief divine does make a threat
to escort chief; another plan is set.

So in the forest, escort turns – attack.
The Bábís, they defend against the pack.

The sole survivor from the lost escort
Mullá Husayn sends back to give report.

And over weeks the Bábís do endure
a number of attacks, defending sure.

And rallying the Bábís to their needs
will Mullá Husayn then cry: "Mount your steeds,
O heroes of God!" And often, thereon
the Bábís cry: "Yá Sáhibu'z-Zamán!" –
humiliate opponents, then move on.

The Grand Vazir gets word of these events.
Successes of the Bábís he resents.

It irks him such a band's advantage gained
while almost all of them not soldier-trained.
They're mostly traders, laborers, divines,
or artisans or students, craftsmen fine –
yet still repeatedly they put to flight
trained military forces filled with fright;
repuls'd and scattered those that they did fight.

But frequent the attacks and treachery
that force Mullá Husayn to seek, and he
does find a refuge – safe for lodging place,
perchance to stop defense and running pace.

October now of 1848,
the shrine of Shaykh Tabarsí is their fate.

The keeper of the shrine, the night before,
did dream a holy man with men of war
did fight heroic battle at the shrine;
the Prophet came and spoke some words sublime.

When he awoke, then saw Mullá Husayn,
he knew this band and dream were one the same;
he tells Mullá Husayn what he did see;
Husayn tells him: "This all will come to be;"
he joins the Bábís most devotedly.

So to accommodate all, they design
the building of a fort around the shrine.

At every stage of their construction chore,
by nearby villagers harassment more,
they often must defend just like before.

While on His way to Tihrán, we do see
Bahá'u'lláh makes way for them to see.

So shortly after building is complete,
Bahá'u'lláh Tabarsí Bábís meet.

While visiting – inspection of the fort,
approving of the work. Now one thing short:

Bahá'u'lláh says one last vital part –
the presence of Quddús to be their heart.
To Mullá Husayn, He then does advise
to seek release of Quddús, now arise.
He recommends they plan for seven men
to go demand release of Quddús when,
the fear of God persuading captor then.

Bahá'u'lláh departs with plan in mind
to there return with more provisions' find.

Quddús is rescued, joins Tabarsí band
in 1848 December. And
Mullá Husayn does openly address
Quddús's higher rank – to all confess –
enhancing the respect and joy from all
for Quddús, who shall lead them through the squall.

Three hundred thirteen at Fort Tabarsí.

The number brings to mind a prophecy
of that same number, when the Last Days come,
who'll be companions of the Promised One.

Bábís just want to live life peacefully.
But Bárfrúsh chief divine won't let it be.
A power-jealous man, he does despise
attraction to the Báb in locals' eyes.
To King he writes and bears a false account,
incites to military action mount
to show the power of the royal court –
destroy and kill the Bábís and their fort.

The Grand Vazir in Tihrán takes the reins
with plan for haughty and despotic gains –
directing now a military surge.
One force after another there converge
until against three-hundred-thirteen men –
an army of twelve-thousand soldiers then
surrounding fort, the Bábís to reduce.
A siege to last for months it does produce.

The Army then begins to mount attacks.
To meet these, Bábí sorties charging back.

The Bábís sally from the fort with zeal
to counter Army blitzes in ordeal.

Each time, attack of Army is repulsed –
the royal soldiers scattered and convulsed.

Besieging forces heavy losses see,
as for their lives do their commanders flee.

Repeatedly the Army-led offense
is met with Bábí foray for defense,
a routing of the Army forces thence.
A cycle days and weeks continues hence.

A massive army, well equipped with best,
supported by the masses, clergy-blessed,
led by the Prince and financed by the State,
approvéd by the King – how can its fate
to be outfought, outwitted, and deterred
by just this band of pious amateurs?

Confounded by this very question too,
the Army then does start on something new.
The cannons are rolled in, of varied size.
They cut off food and water, all supplies.

And as the water level's getting low,
Quddús predicts a rain and then a snow.
And soon thereafter, one and then the next –
a boon for Bábís, Army camp is vexed.
As Nature resupplies the water cache,
the Army site has widespread ruin rash.

Attacks from Army still are the default,
and Bábí forays rush to meet assault –
it's always to repulse the foe's attack,
to parry thrust, disable and push back.

One bad attack, Quddús cries: "Mount your steeds,
O heroes of God!" as he sortie leads.

Mullá Husayn is also in the mix –
the Prince's quarters where his aim does fix.

The Army camp bewildered and confused –
they're routed, their morale is very bruised.

The Prince has fled and hidden from the fray
as Mullá Husayn gains his tent that day;
his own sword damaged, takes the Prince's blade,
then makes his way to where Quddús is laid.

Quddús has been surrounded and was shot.
Husayn and Bábís save him from this lot.

Mullá Husayn does grab Quddús's blade –
a sword in each hand, he a fury made,
and with the Bábís put the camp to flight.
With Quddús they return to fort outright.

To join the Bábís at Fort Tabarsí,
Bahá'u'lláh departs Tihrán with three.
But as toward objective they do fare,
then intercepted and arrested they're.

When punishment is to be meted out,
Bahá'u'lláh does intercede about –
He offers to take everybody's share,
is only one to bastinado bear.
They all are sent back to Tihrán from there.

Each time they do defeat their enemies,
Quddús repeats their purpose as Bábís:

"Repulse assailants, do not punish more.
Protect ourselves, that we'll continue fore
in labors to regenerate mankind –
with no intent for needless harm or bind
to anyone – this purpose keep in mind."

𝕽epeatedly the Bábís, they did try
to urge their foe to let them move on by,
and leave with no more bloodshed they'd apply.

One time Mullá Husayn makes such a plea:
Asks: "Why so cruel? Please let the Bábís be!"
Then shames them for their counter-Islám ways,
so let the Bábís go with no delays.
All this he says with depth and soul of word –
the soldiers moved, some weep at what they heard.

But then commanders order them to fight.
To heavens then does Husayn raise his sight:

"O God!" he cries, "I have completed proof
here to this host, availing no behoof!"

Husayn a rally leads of such account
that moves the Prince, who later does recount:

"That day did he the sword wield in such wise
as to transcend man's power, 'fore our eyes."

One day in early 1849 –
a Mullá Husayn sortie one last time …

… he wakes up, washes, all the cares are gone;
he also puts the Báb's green turban on.

A nameless joy is there upon his face.
Converses long with Quddús in that place.

Throughout the day he's cheering the Bábís.
At midnight, in the morning star he sees
the herald to him of a dawning sight –
eternal union with beloved light.

Next day to counter latest Army thrust,
another foray to repulse they must;
he mounts his charger. Leading Bábí force
does Mullá Husayn speed upon his horse.

"Yá Sáhibu'z-Zamán!" – their cry astounds;
in forest, fort and camp – echo resounds.

Mullá Husayn's the spearhead of the rush;
through seven barricades does he now crush.

As vict'ry brings another day of hope,
his horse gets tangled in some tenting rope.

And as he finds his situation mired,
from in a tree an en'my gun is fired.

Pierced in the chest is Husayn by this deed,
and bleeding now – he's fallen from his steed.
The Bábís take him back to fort with speed.

Quddús is at the fort when they arrive,
as Mullá Husayn's dying but alive.

Quddús now orders privacy within,
and telling all, "Leave me alone with him;
there certain confidential matters are
which I to him alone want to unbar."

The two friends do retreat t'another space.
A Bábí overhears, by door his place.

Quddús most gently, and with greatest love
imparting to his friend the grace above.

With many things that Quddús said, not heard –
attentive Mullá Husayn to his word.
Among what Quddús said, that Bábí heard:

"The hour of departure sped you so,
and left me to the mercy of my foe.
Please God, ere long, be joining you I will –
taste heaven's nameless sweet delights, my fill."

And Mullá Husayn's last words to his friend –
a love and fealty steady to the end:

"A ransom for you, pray my life may be."
And finally, "Are you well pleas'd with me?"

Door opens later, company comes in.
Quddús says, "my farewell I've bade to him.
Things which before I deemed could not be told,
I now have shared with him and did unfold."

Companions enter where he lay in grace –
a faint and peaceful smile upon his face.

Quddús attends to preparation fine,
and buries Mullá Husayn in the shrine.

Interment done, he says to friend Husayn:
"Well is it with you that you did remain
most faithful to God's Covenant till last.
I pray God grant no breach is ever cast
'twixt you and me" - his spirit does forecast.

Thus ends the mortal life of one who'd be
the man who was the first to see – times three:
accept the Báb; the force of Quddús see;
discern Bahá'u'lláh's great Mystery.
Commander filled with valor, chivalry,
devotion, justice and tenacity,
with skill and strength and learning all did see –
"his acts reflected God's ascendancy."

No break for weary grieving friends, alack!
The fort surrounded for a fresh attack.

To counter this did nineteen Bábís go
against two regiments, repulsed the foe;
commander fled, his boot in stirrup still –
he later recollects the Bábís' thrill:
"They came forth with alacrity and joy
to battle. Aye, regardless how employed,
imagination can't conceive the force
behind their valor in the battle's course."

They started with three hundred and thirteen.
A number now have died, the wounded teem;
a few have wavered, leaving fort and fold –
while Army grows and pressures do unfold.

The only nourishment are grass and leaves,
plus adaptations one cannot conceive –
the skin and bone of horses that were slew,
boil'd leather from their saddles and their shoes.

Though famished and exhausted, when attack'd
they'd instantly spring forth to push it back.

Their courage was magnificent to see,
astonishing resistance came to be
borne witness by the Prince and soldiery.

The Army now decides a different ploy
so they their largest cannon can deploy.
A massive tower's built. And placed on top
is cannon whose bombardment will not stop.
The normal cannons, many on the ground.
Fire into heart of fort plus walls to pound.

The outer walls demolished fairly soon.
As well, Quddús emerges from his room –
despite bombardment, great tranquility
while walks to center fort, evinces he.

A cannonball embeds, then rolls his way;
it stops in front of him where he does stay;
he calmly puts his foot atop the ball
then rolls it back and forth, and says to all:

"How utterly oblivious are the
aggressors in their boastfulness, don't see
the power of God's most avenging wrath!
The royal pomp's an empty shadow path.

"Fear not the threats of wicked. Don't dismay
by clamor of ungodly any day.
Each one of you has his appointed hour.
And when your time is done, there is no pow'r
to hasten or retard that time to come –
though all the earth be leagued against just one.
Your life, its span will lessened be by none.
Now should your heart for but one moment see
these booming guns and agitated be,
Divine Protection shall you cast from thee."

These words the Bábís' fearfulness did cease.
Though numbers and provisions did decrease,
their courage and endurance did increase.

But April witnessed how the siege did end.
Bábís not vanquished, nor did yield extend.
But rather by the perfidy of foe,
by brutal treach'ry Army did o'erthrow.

By this time had the King and Grand Vazir
lashed out at Army leaders, giving fear.

The Prince, the uncle of the King, who led,
did see that Bábís clearly felt no dread.

The General had remarked, with all sorties
"new spirit breathed in frames of the Bábís."

"They never will surrender," thus conclude.
But royal court – no understanding mood.
Indeed the King and Vazir now did threat
to punish Army for their failure's debt.

Despairing honest conquest any how,
the Prince conceived a plann'd betrayal now;
he sends a Qur'án copy to the fort,
with note suggesting battle to abort.
An oath on the Qur'án he makes for peace –
and swearing lives and property release
inviolate and spared, Bábís set free –
if they come out dispersing peaceably.

One Bábí says, "what his tongue doth profess,
his heart in truth does not at all confess."

Quddús agrees, thinks treachery somehow –
does kiss the Book, and quotes it open now
with: "O our Lord, decide between us and
between our people with the truth in hand;
the greatest art Thou to decide, command."

Quddús then says to all what he does see,
"by our response, enable them shall we
to show us their intent's sincerity."

Quddús refuses food, knows death is near –
consoles companions now, assuages fear.

"Weep not," he says, "for that which is to come
behind this separating martyrdom:
reunion to be, we can all be sure,
and such as shall eternally endure."

What can be said of what was next to come?
The pen doth falter, hearts to grief succumb ...

Quddús to Prince's camp, he rode his horse.
And out of fort came most of Bábí force –
two-hundred-two, by Prince's promise lured,
while handful in the fort remain secured.

Quddús was then detained by Prince a while,
while massacre that region did defile.

Bábís both in and out of fort were killed.
The volume and the ways the blood was spilled
were not by simple execution done –
but hideous, barbaric acts begun.
Outrageous, horrid on the corpses too –
the bestial hatred of the people do.

Their bodies torn apart or minced by sword,
some fired from cannons as their last reward,
or disemboweled, mutilated, burned,
or tied to trees and bullet-riddle earned.

The forest strewn with desecrate remains.
The fort is plundered, razed and made profane.

Three wealthy Bábís ransomed for a gain.
A few were left for dead, escape attain.
A few more sold as slaves, then freedom gain.

This handful of survivors persevere
to later tell the tale to those who'd hear.

The fate of Quddús –

Christ-like on the whole
– both form of doom that circumstance did dole,
plus virtue and the power of his soul –
enough to transport heart beyond belief
to places mixed with ecstasy and grief.

The Prince forfeits accountability
and hands Quddús to the authority
of chief divine of Bárfurúsh, who had
bloodthirstiness for Quddús, almost mad –
insanely jealous, vicious hatred for
the Bábís, and their two great leaders more.

Quddús in chains paraded through the street,
is jeered and stoned and refuse thrown as greet.

Refined and agonizing tortures next –
the skills of Persian cruelty now get flexed.

And at the height of torment does Quddús
sublime forgiveness and these words produce:

"My God, forgive this people as they stray,
and deal with them with mercy in Thy way.
For verily they do not know what we
do already discover, cherish, see."

In May of 1849, we're there –
Quddús is led to crowded public square...

...by chief divine he's struck down with an axe;
the frenzied mob of Bárfurúsh attacks...

...with every type of tool his flesh is torn
and hacked, dismembered – venting all their scorn;
the thought, much less the sight, cannot be borne...

...his shattered remnants thrown into a fire,
expressing chief divine's triumphant ire...

That night, a different priest, and most humane
collected and did bury his remains.

With such a mortal end did thus move on
th'immortal soul of him bestowed upon
a humble modest man who so perceived
the Beauty Truth Reality received.

The eighteenth Living Letter, "the Last Point,"
"Last Name of God," "Quddús" – these names anoint
companion of the Báb's trip to Hijáz,
brave travel-teacher starting in Shíráz.

Aplomb and honor, piety combine.
A fount of words both potent and sublime.
In-spi-red understanding undefined.
The "hidden treasure" of the Báb to find,
the Báb's reflection, out-of-prison sign.

A leader of the Bábís in the field,
heart-conqu'ring sword of insight did he wield.

A mover of the drama at Badasht,
pretending he with Táhirih had clash'd.

Heroic marshal at Fort Tabarsí.
Bahá'u'lláh equates identity –
in Qur'án mentioned – duty he discharged
as Messenger who with imposture charged.

This heart is filled, but words cannot contain

the light of Quddús and Mullá Husayn.

Eleven months this all did comprehend –
Black Standard raised until Quddús's end.

Nobility supreme the drama feeds.
Incredibly heroic were the deeds –
humiliate and stun in daily course
a vastly overwhelming Army force.

Throughout the siege, the Bábís never would
attempt offensive action when they could.
For not until the Army did attack
would they arise, defend and then push back.

Quddús would this approach reiterate;
at one time also he was heard to state:

"Had we intent of holy war and arms,
the nations we'd convulse, as well alarm.
And thus Muhammad's days would we recall –
the Message thus accepted now by all.
But such is not the way we choose to tread.
Our sole unchanging purpose is instead
to vindicate th'exalted character
of mission high to which our souls refer.
By our own deeds and readiness to shed
our own lifeblood – this is the path we tread.
The time approaches when we meet our fate –
this task and purpose we will consummate."

An episode then closed by treachery,
extinguished with atrocious cru-el-ty ...

... with loss of half of Living Letters; worst:
including both the Last, as well the First.

And of antagonists, what came to be?
The chief divine of Bárfurúsh did see
within a narrow span of time – contracts
a strange disease, without a cure attacks;
he dies in mix of cold and febrile states;
his house neglected and dilapidates –
his property a dump for passers-by,
and mem'ry used whereby to vilify.

Tabarsí's end did crush the Báb with grief –
His broken heart laments beyond relief.
For nine days He refused to see a soul.
A while He does not eat, cannot console.
Five months His Voice is still, with silenced Pen.
A constant rain of tears. And even when
expressions laced with anguish overheard,
and secretary takes down stirring words,
the Báb does those dictations intercept
and has them all destroyed, not to be kept.

Late '49, the Báb, amidst the gloom –
His revelation writing does resume.

First page of writing He does dedicate
to Mullá Husayn, whom He celebrates
with praise; as well Quddús and Tabarsí.
A whole week does He write such eulogy.

The Báb, He summons Sayyáh, a Bábí,
and charges him a task priority:
on His behalf, Sayyáh to visit grave
of both Quddús and Mullá Husayn brave;
on site, invoke and pray there in His place,
collect soil from atop each resting place,
bring back that earth before Naw-Rúz to come,
which He predicts will be His final one.

Sayyáh proceeds to follow this request.
While passing through Tihrán, he stays as guest
Bahá'u'lláh's; Vahíd is also there.
The recent Presence of the Báb does bear;
so to Sayyáh does kneel and kisses feet
is how Vahíd this pilgrim now does greet.

And during this kind visit, there's a job:
Bahá'u'lláh writes letter to the Báb,
which Sayyáh takes back to Him on return –
responding t'which the Báb does write in turn.

The Báb names therewith one Mirza Yayhá –
a younger half-sib of Bahá'u'lláh;
he will be known as "Azal" to Bábís
as well to records of these histories.
The Báb committing Azal to, in there,
Bahá'u'lláh's own tutelage and care.

For here, the Báb agreed to plan comprised
Bahá'u'lláh and someone else advised,
that Azal be appointed nominee
for that expected time which soon will be:
short period that is to intervene
the Báb's own death that clearly is foreseen
until "Him Whom God Shall Make Manifest"
appears and thus fulfills divine behest.

The nomination of Azal would serve
to Bábí continuity preserve,
while also would divert attention from
Bahá'u'lláh, since He had now become
the primal edifying influence
for Bábís; and thus He could still dispense
throughout this int'rim time of consequence.

Despite this nomination, Azal tries
to spend most time in hiding and disguise.

The year of 1850 fully sees
in other parts of Persia more unease.

Religious and the state authorities,
by systematic and intense degrees,
increase the persecution of Bábís.

Within the Capital the rumors fly:
what will the Grand Vazir impending try?

The government severely shocked to see
what happened at the siege of Tabarsí.

And Mirza Taqi Khán, the Grand Vazir –
especially perturbed by what he'd hear:
the time it took a massive army to
a mere three hundred Bábís thus subdue,
and only in the end by trickery.
Distressing is the Bábí "heresy" –
determined now to wipe it out is he.

So in Tihrán the Vazir through his spies
the Bábí meetings infiltrate in guise –
unearthing fifty names for target's aim.
And under pretense of false rumors' claim,
fourteen Bábís are found, and all's distressed.
In home of Kalántar on house arrest –
same home, upstairs, where Táhirih's repressed.

These fourteen were mistreated, tortured too –
'bout other Bábís they revealed no clue.

Frustrated, Grand Vazir declares herewith:
recant their faith, or execute forthwith.

Then seven do recant and are released.
The other seven's staunchness is increased:
refusing to recant, they cause a stir –
the threat of death does not their faith deter.

These seven – well-respected citizens,
in high regard with influential friends.
Some wealthy, others learned divines be.
Of seven do all others in them see
outstanding character, ability –
so much that friends cannot abide this way,
and try to rescue them or ransom pay.

And one of seven poignant now because
he Haji Mirza Siyyid Alí was –
none other than the faithful uncle of
the Báb Himself with most devoted love.
To spare him, Grand Vazir most pointedly
to uncle now gives opportunity:
"Just now recant and we will set you free."

And Mirza Siyyid Alí then replies:
"Denying now the Báb also denies
the character and messages divine
of Moses, Jesus and Muhammad thine,
and ev'ry Prophet, all of them combined.
And so the Báb I never will deny,
and for Him let me be the first to die."

A great crowd gathered in the public square –
the inconceivable to witness there.

Then lifting up his voice and speaking loud,
the uncle of the Báb says to the crowd:

"O people, hear me – offer I myself,
a willing sacrifice.   Hark: you yourself
have for a thousand years expectant prayed
the promised Qá'im's advent undelayed.
And now that He has come, you have consigned
Him to a hopeless exile, and designed
to now exterminate His company.
Were I to ask it now, your destiny
would fill with God's affliction, vengeance, wrath.
However, such is not my chosen path.
Instead, I pray God wipes away your stain
of guilt, and then enables you to gain
awakening from heedlessness, attain."

Then Mirza Siyyid Alí was that day
the first of them to give his life away,
by sword his execution on display.

By what he said and what his death had proved
were many in the crowd so greatly moved.

The executioner was shaken sore,
he stepped away and then came back no more.

Replacement executioner steps in
to punishment of other six begin.

The final words these martyrs did employ –
defiant statements, or ecstatic joy,
their challenges and eloquent appeals,
forgiving persecutors in ordeal,
whatever carried with their final breath
as they did face and meet with joy their death –
did minds of many in the crowd enthrall,
and also did it shake the hearts of all.

The bodies of the seven in the square,
so citizens by thousands passing there
may curse, or mock, or spit, or kick, or stone,
or refuse on their bodies heaped and thrown –
indignities to make the angels moan.

Already mourning over Tabarsí,
now from this news the Báb weeps grievously.
In honor of their martyrdom He wrote
a Tablet, calling them the "Seven Goats" –
invoking a Tradition known, wherein
an image: seven goats who walk therein
before the Qá'im – Judgment Day will see.
Perhaps foreseeing what is soon to be.

Embodying most high nobility
in face of the most hateful perfidy –
when countrymen do show the worst of traits,
the best of attributes they demonstrate,
those virtues that could make their nation great,
redounding to true glory of Írán –
thus were the Seven Martyrs of Tihrán.

The heart and pen now almost cannot bear
continuing the stories of elsewhere.

The themes of Nayríz and Zanján we see
are recapitulating Tabarsí.

from moment of acceptance was Vahíd
a vig'rous travel teacher – word and deed.

To many towns he'd visit in Írán,
and then he ended up in Kurdistán,
till circumstances in Mázindarán;
he then began to head to Tabarsí
to with Quddús and Mullá Husayn be.

But by the time he reach'd Tihrán, 'twas clear
the siege prevented all from coming near.

So visit with Bahá'u'lláh did he,
which strengthened him in spirit nat'rally.
Although already capable was he
– unrivall'd knowledge and capacity –
yet being with Bahá'u'lláh did show
his knowledge and devotion more did grow.

From there he went to Qum and then Káshán,
then other cities after Isfáhán –
applying fervor and ability
attracting many, teaching dauntlessly.

Then ending up in Yazd where hot and dry
and one of his three residences lie –
a town where he's respected everywhere,
his wife and four sons then residing there.

In early 1850 comes to place –
his mansion beautiful becomes his base
for earnest teaching. Visitors do throng,
believers swell, and opposition strong.

Because of his promotion of the Báb,
his home's attacked by soldiers and a mob.
One foolish Bábí disobeys Vahíd –
retaliates, more danger from his deed.

Vahíd advises Bábís to leave town.
And tells his wife their house will soon come down –
'twas built to be demolished for this Cause,
belongings meant to sacrifice, no pause.
With two sons to her father's town she goes,
and he with other two, a plan he chose.
As he predicted, nothing could avoid –
the mansion soon was plundered and destroy'd.

Then he and two began to make their way
toward Nayríz, their second home to stay.

In every village on their route he'd teach
and stay a while if open minds he'd reach,
or move on if no int-er-est he sees,
till finally they do approach Nayríz.

From his own residential quarter came
entire population with acclaim

to welcome him, despite the gov'nor's threats.
In fact, in gov'nor's heart it fear begets;
and governor does leave the village then –
in outskirts moves into a fortress den.

Vahíd goes to the mosque immed'ately
to clarify intent for all to see:

"I'm only here to share the Cause of God.
For chance to touch your hearts do I thank God.
But I don't plan to stay, for your own sakes,
for fear that it will for you danger make."

The people did insist for him to stay.
Attraction of more people every day.

An Army of one thousand gov'nor breeds
to suddenly attack and seize Vahíd.

Vahíd instructs some Bábís as resort –
abide and reinforce a nearby fort.

The governor attacks the Bábí lair.
As Vahíd joins, now seventy-two there.

And with a credo same as Tabarsí –
defend, do not attack philosophy –
they still repulse the Army easily.

The gov'nor calls Shíráz to bring help in,
and thus a siege protracted does begin.

A parallel dynamic in Zanján:
'twas fiercest persecution in Írán.

Home of Hujjat, May 1850 sees
the largest of attacks against Bábís.

And leading up to it was the divines'
hostility increasing over time.

Hujjat, before he even was Bábí,
his thought and way free from orthodoxy –
outspoken, critical of the divines,
he's erudite and eloquent of mind,
convincing to disciple and to peer,
evoked opposing cries from those who fear.

Moreso was this when he became Bábí –
Zanján divines with hate now want to see
his downfall, nay destruction come to be.

In Tihrán, house arrest he came to be,
unable to join up at Tabarsí.

But chance he had Bahá'u'lláh to see,
which greatly strengthened his capacity.

In 1850 to Zanján returns.
The smold'ring hatred from divines now burns,
awaiting smallest incident to show,
and spark a conflagration that would grow.
Indeed that spark and chance came for the foe.

Between some children, minor quarrel came.
Hujjat does intervene within the same,
protecting Bábí child, it does inflame –
becomes the target of the clergy blame.

To gov'nor, clergy fail to take Hujjat.
So torture, kill his friend instead of that.

The governor decides that all Zanján
must choose a side 'twixt Bábís and Islám.

The town is split 'tween Hujjat and divines,
with geographic separating lines.

The Bábí following – three thousand strong –
within a fortress, refuge takes the throng.

The government, with twenty-thousand men
attack, besiege the Bábís in their pen.

These two more sieges seem beyond relief.
The news of them does bring the Báb more grief.

At this point He does gather up His things –
His writings, pen-case, plus His seals and rings –
and sending to Bahá'u'lláh did do.
Along with these, a scroll of paper blue.

Upon this scroll, in most exacting pen,
a craftsmanship beyond the normal ken.

The blue scroll that Bahá'u'lláh received –
the Báb's exquisite penmanship conceived
a pentacle within which is perceived
500 derivations of "Bahá" –
calligraphy to praise Bahá'u'lláh.

Back in Nayríz, Vahíd and company
are recapitulating Tabarsí:
do not attack, repulse effectively.

The Army – heavy losses do they see.
And once again the Army strategy
is in the end to win with treachery.

The military leader writes a note
and sends it to Vahíd; within he wrote
proposal for Vahíd to come explain
the Báb and what His teachings do contain.
A promise on Qur'án the man does state
sincerely to the claims investigate;
if truth in Cause, accepted it will be;
if not, a safe return to fort gets he,
and conflict then resuming thus will be.

Vahíd and others go to Army base,
three days they're entertained with lavish face.

Vahíd then forced to write to Bábí fort
that says a settlement was reached resort;
he tries to send a second letter too
disclosing truth, but that did not get through.

The Bábís exit fort, are seized and chained –
appalling torture, killing unrestrained.

The fort was razed, with many houses smashed,
and wives and children taken unabashed,
abominably treated and in fear.
The heads of dead were stuffed with straw, on spear.
All taken to Shíráz with public jeer.

'Tis not the end how hateful did react
as Vahíd's house and city-quarter sacked,
extorting money from the residents –
contrasts depravity and innocence.

Vahíd is tied to horse by turban green,
his emblem of descent from Prophet seen –
is dragged through streets, and stoned, and beaten dead,
then trampled into dust where all do tread.

'Tis now in 1850, month of June.
The Grand Vazir sees happening so soon ...

... events in Tihrán, Nayríz, Zanján three
are following the siege at Tabarsí ...

... Alarm'd severely, badly shaken he ...

... The failures ... Haji Mirza Aqasi ...

... A danger to the State has come to be.

He will not dare attempt his path preferred –
triumphant was the Báb last time 't'occurred.
Too risky to attempt again to meet
through argument divines the Báb defeat.

Instead he must destroy completely now
the Bábí movement from the core, somehow.

So taking his decision, he decrees.
Again, the Báb is taken to Tabríz.

When to Tabriz the Báb was taken He,
the Gov'nor saw to hospitality –
respect, consideration, courtesy.

And three days after His arrival here
did come the brother of the Grand Vazir,
prime minister's commandment to convey
to execute the Báb that very day.

A public execution it's to be,
and anyone who claims to be Bábí
will also thereby executed be.

The Governor declines to be a part.
Before the plan's momentum falls apart,
Vazir's instructions to his brother say
to carry out the order, no delay.

The Báb, as well His secretary with,
to barracks of the city moved forthwith.

Intending that His dignity be ripp'd,
the Báb of sash and turban He is stripp'd.

They're led on foot along the city streets
where turmoil and a throng the Pris'ner greets.

At one point during this procession loud,
a haggard young man pushes through the crowd,
and at the Báb's feet does himself he throw –
to hem of clothes he clutches, will not go.

"O Master! Send me not from Thee!" he cries.
"Wherever Thou dost go," he then applies,
"do suffer me to follow Thee," he sighs.

The Báb says:
                    "Muhammad Alí, arise
and rest assured tomorrow shall your eyes
then witness that which God has now devised,
and you will be with Me, does fate comprise."

The Báb re-names this man – "Anís" is he.
Two others do confess their loyalty.
All five into a cell consigned would be.

For years before the current scene did show,
Anís had prior been devoted so;
his uncle had been first to Máh-Kú go;
his father vi'lently oppos'd belief,
and locked Anís in house with no relief,
thus causing him to supplicate in grief,
especially when twice the Báb would be
within Tabríz, and Anís wished to see.

One night amidst, Anís did have a dream:
the Báb appear'd to him in his extreme.
Therein the Báb says His own martyrdom
there in Tabríz is surely soon to come,
and to Anís a promise does make He –
compan'on of His Martyrdom he'll be.

Anís's grief to joy it was transformed.
"Tell this to nobody," his uncle warned.

Anís's calm contentment did increase,
that father from the house-lock did release –
until this very day, weeks later now.
The circumstances fav'rable somehow
that when to Tabríz now the Báb was brought,
Anís did rush from house, his Master sought.

Now with His secretary and these three –
the Báb, within the barrack cell is He.

He knows the next day, He will surely die.
His mood that night before, content and high –
they saw His face did glow with joy unique.
To cheer and soothe compan'ons did He speak.

"Tomorrow is the day, My martyrdom.
If one of you might now arise, do come
and with his own hand end My life forthwith.
Prefer do I to now be slain therewith
by hand of friend instead of enemy."

His cell mates did refuse, wept bitterly –

– except for Anís who sprang forward to
then do aught that the Báb would ask to do.

The other cell mates, horrified were they –
and made Anís rescind this right away.
The Báb then interjected and did say:

"This same youth who has risen to comply
with My wish will together with Me die.
My martyrdom – the Will of God come down;
him will I choose to share with Me its crown."

Next morning, early and quite hastily,
the Báb was to be taken out to see
some of the head divines, and to obtain
their written auth'rization to be slain.

Already early morning do we see
the Báb now talks with His secretary –
instructions quite important now gives He.

The Báb tells him: "Your own faith don't confess;
thereby you'll be enabled to address
when your time comes, and thereby to convey
to those who'll hear you what you see today;
and things which now just you know, then you'll say."

And while some more instructions He does share,
the chief attendant of the jail comes there
and interrupts the conversation – yea,
he scolds the secretary for delay.

The Báb then clearly, calmly does He say:

"Not till I've said to him all of those things
that I do wish to say, can anything,
not any earthly power silence Me.
Though all the world against Me arméd be,
yet powerless shall they be to deter
intention Mine, till last word does occur."

The chief attendant knew not what to say.
Though startled, still led both of them away.

On both the Báb and Anís, now we see
their necks and wrists with iron fetters be.
Long cords are through the iron collars fed.
By these through streets and market places led.

The crowd tremendous presses and exults
to glimpse and hurl out refuse and insults.

To place of the divines they did attain.
The priests refuse to see the Báb again;
already was His sentence signed and sealed.
But to persuade Anís they had appealed
for him to save himself and now recant,
to which Anís replied he surely shan't
and never will deny the Báb. Indeed,
Anís berated the divines to heed
that they are mad themselves to thus allow
the killing of the promised Qá'im now.

And then, returning to the barracks square,
to Sám Khán they are handed over there.

Sám Khán, the col'nel of the regiment
to now the execution implement.

Though ordered were the soldiers and this man,
misgivings had Sám Khán about this plan;

Armenian and Christian were they all –
reluctant with the execution call.

Sám Khán was moved by what he'd seen and heard
about the Báb's behavior and His words.
And ill at ease is he, indeed afraid
if execution by his hand is made,
'twill bring down wrath of God upon his head;
to carry order out, reluctant dread.

Sám Khán goes to the Báb and tells Him true:
"I entertain no ill will against you" –
confesses his reluctance and his fear,
he further pleads his case with heart sincere:
he says, "if your cause be the Cause of Truth,
enable me to free myself, forsooth,
from obligation of your blood to shed" –
alternative he sought from this instead.

The Báb does calm the col'nel there and then,
and reassures him with a promise, when

says:
"follow your instructions"
to him clear,

"and if your own intention be sincere,
then surely the Almighty – able's He
to you relieve from your perplexity."

Eyewitnesses were many; testified

to what then followed, stunned and mystified.

The two were taken to the barrack square –
ten thousand the onlookers gathered there.

The Báb and Anís tied together were.
On wall of military barracks were
suspended both by ropes.
And then request
by Anís: put his head on the Báb's chest,
to shield Him from full force of bullets' thrust –
a final act of sacrificial trust.

The crowd not only filled the barrack square,
but cramm'd the roofs of barracks, houses there.

The seven-hundred-fifty soldiers stand
in three files of two-hundred-fifty, and
one line behind the other, rifle each –
the regiment drawn up in ready reach.

Then one row at a time, the firing squad
took aim and fired. Noise deaf'ning filled the quad,
as did the gun smoke, shrouding all in dark.

Anticipated, dreaded end –

but hark!

Smoke lifting,   the suspense of public swelled,

astonished were at what they all beheld.

Incredulous, the onlookers did see
Anís stood upright, unconcernedly,
unscathed, untouched – and smiling standing there.

And no sign of the Báb now in the square !

They cry with awe, or fear, or with delight:

"Siyyid-i-Báb has vanished from our sight!"

The rifle bullets – seven-fifty all –
just severed ropes that bound them to the wall!

A gen'ral uproar quickly breaking out –
officials running to and fro and shout.

A frenzied search ensues – and what to tell?
The chief attendant finds Him in His cell!

The same lock'd room He'd been the night before,
same conversation He was in before –
the Báb – unhurt, untouched, unruffled He –
no sign of any bullet mark to see.

In conversation calmly now is He –
last charge to finish with secretary.

Attendant chief's bewilderment does brim,
he's frightened as the Báb now says to him:

"My conversation I have finished now;
you may proceed, fulfill your purpose now."

In light of rifle's nature in those days –
their imprecision, worse in smoky haze –
plus massive total bullets volley'd forth –
for all these reasons, others to set forth –
impossibly, all seven-fifty shots
touch'd nothing but to cut the ropes and knots!

In awe and terror, chief attendant fled –
resigned his post immed'ately from dread.

With greater awe, Sám Khán did then refuse
in aught that might the Báb harm or abuse.
Yea, even if it costed his own life,
his men he ordered then away from strife.

The regiment Armenian took heart,
refusing to take any further part.
The crowd – near pandemonium did start.

The brother of the Grand Vazir did see
how fickle now the Tabríz mob could be.
At one time did they hail the Báb, and then
another time denounced Him, now again
they might cry miracle beyond their ken.
Preempting this, the brother hastily
assembles Muslim regiment, to be
the second firing squad this day will see.

Again, the Báb and Anís are tied up.

Again, three files of soldiers are lined up.

This time the Báb addressed the multitude –
His verdict on Tabríz He does conclude:

"O wayward generation! Don't you see?
Your chosen way, had you believed in Me,
would sacrifice in My Path, and forsooth
would follow the example of this youth
who ranks above the most of you in truth.
The day will come when you recognize Me.
That day, with you I shall have ceased to be."

The second seven-fifty shots are fired.

Unprecedented is what then transpired.

The very moment bullets hit their mark
and bodies of the two are shattered stark,
exceptionally vi'lent gale arose
and swept across the city. Whirlwind blows
to circulate a cloud of dust so dense
to blind their eyes, obscure the sunlight thence.
The darkness lasted noon to nightfall. This
a multitude did openly witness.

Shíráz nearby an earthquake did sustain.
For city, turmoil; people, havoc reign.
Plus cholera and famine can't contain.

The Báb and Anís – flesh are blended one;
forsooth insep'rable had they become.

The visage of the Báb – unmark'd and clean ...
Expression on His face – calm and serene ...

July the 9th of 1850, Noon –
His earthly life was ended much too soon –
within the thirty-first year of His age –
His seventh year of ministry engaged.

What are among the signs we may descry

from Trumpet First of when God passes by?

Thus ends a life of which posterity
will view as standing at convergency
of two prophetic cycles protean –
First: stretching back to dawning soul of Man;
The next: propelling 'cross time's unborn reach,
where progress transcends current thought or speech.

Apotheosis such a life attained,
its consummating martyrdom sustained –
unparalleled in annals of the lives
of Great Ones where Religion all derives.

Within a year, one-third of firing squad
that made the kill – in earthquake met their God.

Within three years, the rest for mutiny
by firing squad did meet their destiny –
their corpses lanced to meet indignities
of gazing crowd on street-sides of Tabríz.

Within two years of the Báb's final breath,
the Grand Vazir and brother met their death.

Remains of the two martyrs – we will see,
their future fate – itself an odyssey.

The mayor of Tabríz and one Bábí
retrieve the bodies for their dignity
from careless watch of guarding soldiery –
becomes a gift to all posterity.

Remains were sealed in casket, safely hid.
Directed by Bahá'u'lláh, they did
remain in hiding, going place to place.
Believers move them 'round the city space.

In 1890, forty years gone by
determine where remains will fin'lly lie.
Bahá'u'lláh Himself points out the site
in Holy Land, dust sacred to alight;
instructs His son to finish this – a must –
the final resting spot for hallow'd dust.

'Abdu'l-Bahá – Bahá'u'lláh's own son
completed what Bahá'u'lláh'd begun:
did purchase land of site, and did pursue
construction of a mausoleum true;
and also did direct through years with pains
the secret transfer of the Báb's remains
within Írán from town to city, and
then ultimately to the Holy Land.

And once the mausoleum was complete,
1909 when seven decades meet,
'Abdu'l-Bahá with own hands did the feat –
interr'd the Báb at final resting place.
Mount Carmel, Haifa cradles sacred space.

Shoghi Effendi, 1953,
the grandson of 'Abdu'l-Bahá, then he
completes the superstructure over shrine –
a place of light and beauty for all time.

White marble skirt supports an octagon,
a drum atop, tall 18 windows on,
each window for a Living Letter's love,
the crown a golden dome does gleam above,
sublime the timeless garden does surround –
on mountainside the mystic does abound,
looks over bay to Medit'ran'an Sea,
to welcome pilgrims wher'ver they may be.

From all over the world do people come
on pilgrimage, pay homage to the One
Who heralded the breaking of the Dawn
when tableau for humanity redrawn,
and laid the groundwork for a whole new stage
in human evolution – mystic Age
that soon will culminate, at God's behest,
when comes "Him Whom God Shall Make Manifest" –
for Whom Alí, the Báb, did give His all.
Mayhap the people then will heed His call.

The "Qá'im" from Whom prophecies resolve ...

the "Point round which the Messengers revolve" ...

the "Great Announcement" Who did raise the call,

"from Whom proceeds the knowledge full of all" ...

the "Morn of Truth" to "banish shades of night,"

as well the "Harbinger of Most Great Light" ...

"Elijah's" and the "Baptist John's" "return" ...

the "Ushídar-Máh" Zoroastr'ans yearn ...

"First Trumpet Blast," the "Second Woe," "Mihdí" ...

the "Mystic Fane" and "Sea of Seas" was He ...

the "Primal Point that generates all things" ...

forecast of many Faiths – fulfillment brings

to end "Prophetic Cycle" where we've been –

the "Cycle of Fulfillment" to begin.

𝔑𝔬𝔴𝔥𝔢𝔯𝔢 except in Gospels can be found
Religion-Founder's death that does resound
with martyrdom of Prophet of Shíráz –
so inexplicable that moment was.
Phenomenon eyewitness'd and confirmed
by masses, government who both affirmed,
as well by those with standing recognized,
historians who saw it with their eyes.

Such undisputed marvelous event,
reflecting unique potency 'twas sent
in life of Báb and death and mission done.
No parallel is found except for one –
the passion of the Christ and ministry.
Remarkable the similarity
'twixt Jesus and the Báb for all to see –
their persons and respective history,
the charact'ristics, archetypes, events,
such parallels of num'rous incidents –
predicting an unfolding destiny
to effloresce, the future's eyes to see.

The Báb did sublimate this destiny
within one larger than the Faith Bábí.

The Báb did sublimate this destiny
within one larger than the Faith Bábí.

Not only independent Author be
of Dispensation God-reveal'd was He,
but also Herald of New Era was.
Inaugurator of New Cycle does
precede a soon-to-come Revealer, Who
will manifest awaited Spirit True,
Whose cycle will encompass eons forth
– the flower-fruit of what the Báb brought forth.

Extr'ordinary circumstance relate:
the Martyrdom that day did stimulate
a widespread int'rest to investigate
His story, message He did promulgate.

An int'rest keen among the Persians, and
as well outside the confines of the land –
from Europeans living in Írán
to their contemporaries out beyond.

In Western Europe, Russia, words were fond –

officials, scholars, merchants, publicists,
advisers, diplomats and journalists,
divines and travelers' concern enlists,
and even could a monarch not resist.

Opin'ons of these people, they would say:
this phenom – most important of this Day ...

this "hero" of "humanity," He stood
steadfast for "universal brotherhood,"
for "concord" and for "justice" and for good ...

His "love" and "courage" marked for all to see ...
"the finest product of his country" – He ...

His "sacrifice" for people, leaving self ...
His "martyrdom" a "miracle" itself ...

"true God-man" – "more than prophet" or a sage...
they'd say He was the "Jesus of the Age" ...

while others spoke His place in history:
"religious mov'ment most important" be
"since genesis of Christianity."

So many did from all parts of the world
set out for Persia, see what had unfurled.

Soon int'rest spread in Europe rapidly
in circles of the arts, diplomacy,
and intellectual, literary.

"All Europe stirred," one publicist did write,
"to pity, indignation" for this plight.

Soon poems, articles, a play did come
about the Báb as well His martyrdom –
perform'd, translated, publish'd – public roused.
Ideals for which He lived and died espoused.
E'en sympathy was genuine aroused
and int'rest of renownéd Tolstoy, who
himself did pen a commentary too.

But execution of the Báb, along
with death or prison for all leaders strong,
deprives the Mov'ment of the leadership
to now endure the persecutor's whip
or to maintain the full integrity
of standards of behav'or, clarity
of purpose, vision that the Báb had taught.
With danger the Community is fraught.

The Dispensation of the Báb thus ends.
Such peril and potential it portends.

The whole of Persia, for a brief time range,
stood on the brink of widespread social change.

Divisions and the moral bankruptcy
of civic and religious hierarchy,
along with cyclic civil disarray,
the weakness of the monarchy that day,
susceptibility of public mind –
these fertile circumstances all combined
with leading Bábís' what the world did see
of their exceptional ability,
as well of course and most especially
the Báb's phenomenal capacity.

These mix – a situation to create
that, had He chosen to control the State,
few doubted that the Báb He could have seized
the pow'r political, rule as He pleased.
Especially – if He did but accept
the offers to assist so urgent kept
by powerful men like Manúchihr Khán –
the Báb could have, as many thought foregone,
establish self as Master of Írán.

Indeed the precedent already set,
as Shí'ih-Persian principles beget
that Shah is merely regent – held kingdom
in trust for the Mihdí until He'd come.

And since the Báb did make the Qá'im claim,
convincing many Persians of acclaim,
Shí'ih tradition did require the King
with care, respect – the claims examining.

Though Grand Vazir and higher clergy did
behind their own positions fearful hid,
and interfered for such a meeting did –
yet had the Báb demanded audience
and took assistance offered for defense,
a fully diff'rent outward outcome thence.

And yet the Báb refused such show of force,
predicting it would cost His life in course –
thereby affirming peaceable His course,
and full reliance on the Spirit's force
as sole support and vindication of
His mission, message – justice, truth and love.

He magnetized the lives and souls and minds
with potency in being of three kinds:
the spirit of His character was first;
then mastery religious unrehearsed;
then social message, revolution burst.

His love, compassion and humility,
combined with justice and nobility,
along with ample human quality –
a charm and irresistible effect
on all but those who hatefully object.

His mastery both effortless and true,
both unassuming and in open view,
of topics, questions of religious mind –
theology or jurisprudence kind,
belief or prophecy, abstruse or clear,
or those that would bring controversy near.
Spontaneous composing would astound,
the lucid depth of His ideas confound.

Extr'ordinary that a man so young
and little vers'd in fields of learning done,
could unrehearsed so easily reply –
confounding ranking theologians by,
inspiriting His hearers all thereby.

And even so, the Báb did minimize
the future of such studies in His eyes.

Indeed what He did strongly emphasize
was social purpose on which future lies –
which His own Person and His knowledge served,
and everyone's attention it deserved.

The Shí'ih Persia culture as it was –
in fatalistic obscurantist fuzz,
and isolated from surrounding climes,
with little change there since Med'eval times.

Within the setting of a Muslim State
that regulates all things from small to great,
assumed that the Mihdí's expected role
included to uplift a person's soul
but also nation-changing as a whole.

The Báb, as Mihdí, thus create did He
a full new concept of society.

While tapping faith and culture from the past,
yet breaking mold and whole new one recast –
did capture loyalty with hope for change
for tens of thousands 'cross the social range.

A nearly crit'cal mass did motivate.
The edge of nation-change did propagate.

From populace to King, He made the call
to follow Him, new Persia make for all.

Did principles and laws elucidate
for new society – the Bábí State –
its public matters, peace, security,
its social structures and economy,
e'en international diplomacy.

Along with this collective system, He
for personal religiosity
did also thus reveal a panoply
of disciplines and moral precepts, and
prophetic guidance gen'ral from His hand.

Deliberately strict these teachings were,
to break from Muslim frame t'which all refer,
and marshal the believers' deepest soul –
participate in new historic role.

This role – the overarching theme that He
did write throughout Bayán most lib'rally:
transform Írán as prelude, to prepare
for Most Great Being, Who would soon show there –
God's Universal Manifestation
Who'll take the change beyond that one nation.

The Báb did see His Faith unusual –
His Dispensation: pure transitional.

The Báb, though independent Prophet He,
did manifest Divine for all to see,
a Messenger with Revelation free,
and own religious Dispensation be
with epochal potentiality –
yet would the Báb take all this potency,
to channel and to concentrate its force
in narrowed time and space, to chart a course
to change a single nation rapidly
instead of widespread over centuries ...

... in prep for when the world would soon be bless'd,
emerge "Him Whom God Shall Make Manifest" –
the One whom *all* religions do await,
the One to Whom the Báb was just "the Gate,"
about Whom verses of the Báb did sing:
on that One's Hand the Báb was just a ring.

For this One had the Báb His Cause unfurled,
the Promised One – Írán will soon be swirled,
His Message will be carried through the world.

When "Him Who God Shall Manifest" appears,
He'll bring a Revelation with no peers.
For coming Age the teachings He'll reveal,
and choose from Bayán what keep, what repeal.
Decide He will what parts, if any, from
the Bábí System will retained become.

The time that Promised One was to appear –
the Báb did indicate the time was near.
Though He refused to state precisely when,
He told some followers that they would then
in their own lifetime meet the Promised One,
and serve Him when His ministry's begun.

The Báb did state no one could falsely claim
to be the Promised One and it sustain;
so don't oppose if one does claim advance –
hold peace, God to His will show, give the chance.

The Báb in the Bayán and elsewhere too
did sometimes make a cryptic ref'rence to
"the year nine" and sometimes "the year nineteen" –
and at the time the meaning was not seen.

And so the purpose of the Bábí State
would have been to collectively create
a large enlightened culture – matrix be –
effective harmonized society,
to be environment and agency
with readiness and with capacity
to recognize, receive and propagate
large-scale, wholesale and with a rapid rate,
as well throughout the world to then relate
the Message, also the appearance great
of "Him Who'll Manifest," the Promised One –
within but decades, very soon to come.

This vision and potential did abort
before it could be realized – cut short
by martyrdom of Mihdí in His prime,
and Bábí leaders too before their time,
and further thwarted by the massacre
of thousands of Bábís that did occur
in country-widespread reign-of-terror's blur.

Despite this, still the possibility:
united and distinct community.
Though smaller maybe, still it could be strong,
the purpose of the Báb to move along.
Upright, perceptive, new life-pattern use
to still embrace, embody and diffuse
the will of "Him Whom God Will Manifest" –
thereby fulfilling then the Báb's behest.

VOLUME

TWO

the rising of the Splendor of the Sun

Mírzá Husayn-Alí – Bahá'u'lláh

TO BE CONTINUED …

66892167R00133

Made in the USA
Lexington, KY
27 August 2017